PRIMITIVE TECHNOLOGY

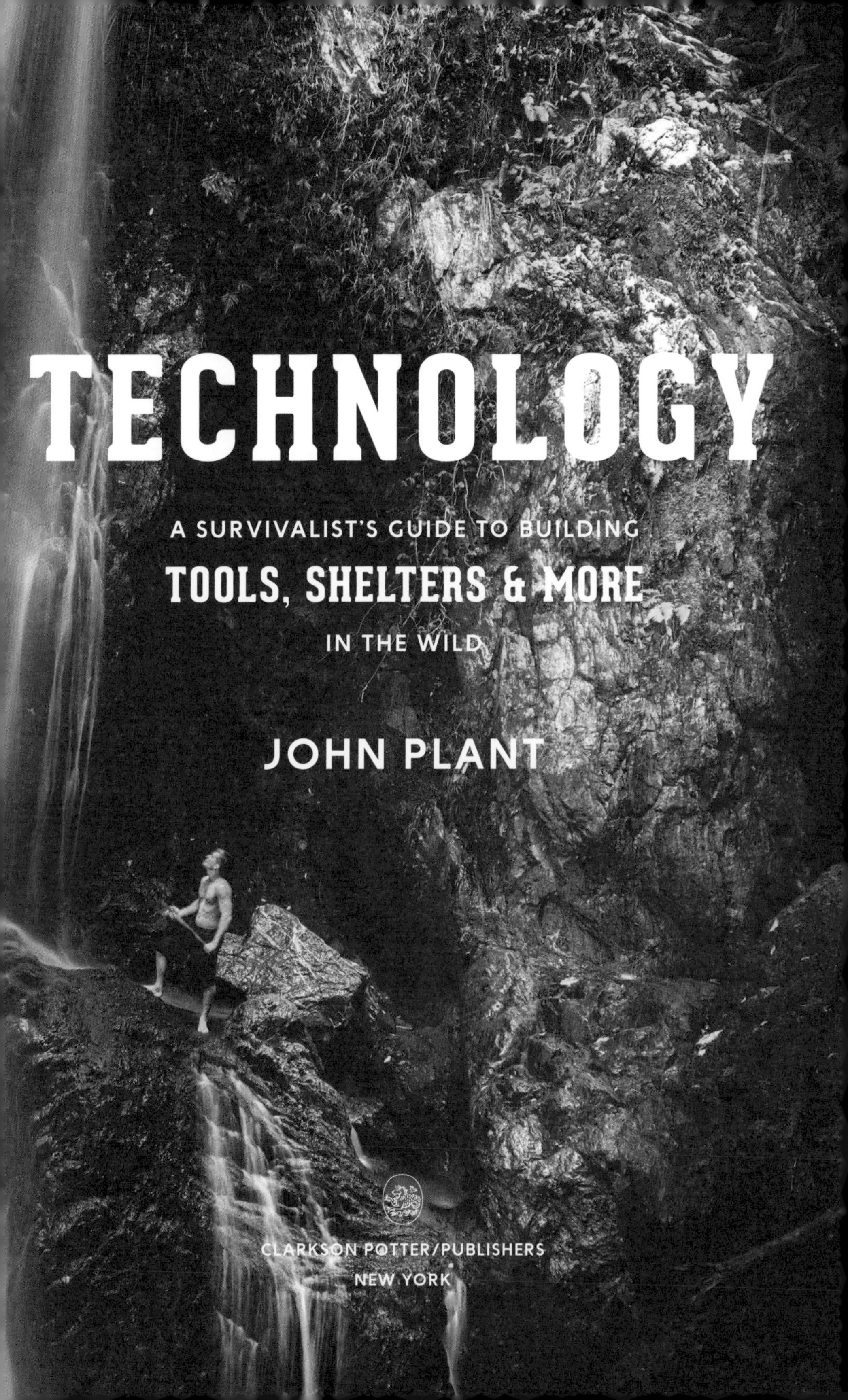

TECHNOLOGY

A SURVIVALIST'S GUIDE TO BUILDING
TOOLS, SHELTERS & MORE
IN THE WILD

JOHN PLANT

CLARKSON POTTER/PUBLISHERS

NEW YORK

Copyright © 2019 by John Plant
Step-by-step photographs © 2019 by John Plant
All other photographs copyright © 2019 by Ben Neale
Illustrations copyright © 2019 by Zachary Smith

Published in the United States by Clarkson Potter/Publishers,
an imprint of Random House, a division of Penguin Random
House LLC, New York. clarksonpotter.com

CLARKSON POTTER is a trademark and POTTER with
colophon is a registered trademark of Penguin Random
House LLC.

Library of Congress Cataloging-in-Publication Data
is available.

ISBN 978-1-9848-2367-0
Ebook ISBN 978-1-9848-2368-7

Printed in China

Book design by Jen Wang
Cover ilustration by Zachary Smith

10 9 8 7 6

First Edition

CONTENTS

BEFORE WE BEGIN 9
INTRODUCTION 11

BASIC TOOL KIT

HAMMER STONE 14

STONE BLADES 16

HAND AXE 18

DIGGING STICK 20

MALLET & CHISEL 22

HEAT

FIRE STICKS 28

BOW DRILL 30

BLOWPIPE 34

WOODEN TONGS 38

BURN BOWL 40

HUNT

BOW 46

FISH TRAP 50

SPEAR THROWER 54

SLING 58

CLOTHING & TEXTILES

STANDARD WEAVE BASKET 64

COIL WEAVE BASKET 68

TWINING WEAVE BASKET 72

CORDAGE 76

DROP SPINDLE 78

LOOM 80

SANDALS 84

ADVANCED TOOL KIT

ADZE 90

CELT AXE 94

CORD DRILL 98

WATER HAMMER 104

SHELTER

DRYSTONE WALL 112

MUD WALL 116

WATTLE & DAUB WALL 120

DOME HUT 126

GABLED ROOF HUT 132

A-FRAME HUT 140

ROUND HUT 146

PYRAMIDAL HUT 152

CHIMNEY 156

ONDOL 160

PRIMITIVE PYROTECHNOLOGY

REUSABLE CHARCOAL MOUND 166

IRON PRILLS 172

UPDRAFT KILN 176

NATURAL DRAFT FURNACE 182

FORGE BLOWER 186

ACKNOWLEDGMENTS 192

BEFORE WE BEGIN

I wrote this book for entertainment purposes only. If you follow any of the projects here, please exercise extreme caution:

→ Always respect the local laws, especially regarding trespassing and conservation.

→ Take special care when lighting fires, observing landscape and weather conditions before you begin. Fires can cause destruction to life, property, and the environment. Note the amount of dry fuel lying around and wind speed. Clear a 3.5-foot (1 m) radius of flammable debris around furnaces and fire pits.

→ Never aim your weapons toward other people or property. If you do practice with homemade projectile weapons, do so out of range of developed areas where your weapon could cause damage.

→ If you need land for practicing your primitive technology, and you do not own it, be sure to ask permission of the landowners. Also, consult local land-use laws regarding public land. You might have to get creative: A farmer may allow you to use their land in exchange for the buildings you create. Or perhaps you start a co-op or club with other members so you can all pitch in to pay for a land lease.

→ Nature is tough, so take personal care of yourself. Think about each activity you are about to take part in. Hot coals can cause serious burns when stepped on. Wild animals can cause injury or death, and you can acquire diseases through open wounds or by ingesting contaminated food and water. Even breaking up sticks can pose a risk of injury to the eyes. Research potential dangers before entering the environment and take careful measures to avoid them.

→ Lastly, take care of the environment. Be responsible when using natural resources. Don't overuse the natural flora and fauna. Selectively use pest species over native ones where possible. Always leave enough plants and animals to grow and reproduce so that there will be more for the next generations to enjoy.

INTRODUCTION

Primitive technology is the practice of making tools, structures, textiles, and clothing using only natural materials found in the wild. The goal of this pastime is to revisit disciplines and skills that modern technology has made obsolete. Some of the projects in this book are based on techniques used in primitive times; others are drawn from my own experiences with outdoors crafting.

Growing up in a rural area of Australia's Far North Queensland, I had an interest in science but no access to the latest technology. The systems and techniques our ancestors used to secure the basic amenities humans have always needed for survival – food, clothing, and shelter – intrigued me. I became preoccupied by the idea of making implements from scratch and living in the wilderness without contemporary resources. As most children do, I built small forts using sticks and stones; once I mastered rudimentary skills I tackled more complex structures and techniques. The next step was to film the building process, and I created a YouTube channel for all the videos. I knew that others might enjoy my hobby as much as I did, but I didn't anticipate how popular the channel would become, and I'm grateful to everyone who has supported it.

This book is a collection of projects featured on my YouTube channel, each one tested and refined over my years of honing the skills of primitive technology. The instructions and information on materials detailed in this book will help you to make them yourself. Most of the materials I use are native to Australia, so where possible I've suggested substitutions, but I encourage you to experiment with whatever you find in the wild. The level of difficulty ranges from easy (a few steps or materials) to complicated. If primitive technology is new to you, I recommend working with a partner on the more advanced projects.

In this book, you'll read about the projects I came up with for my channel. One particularly vexing obstacle I had to deal with involved animal products. Because of the legal restrictions on hunting in Australia, I had to come up with alternatives for bone and leather, which was especially difficult for some projects. For example, it would have been much easier to make a bellows out of leather instead of clay, wood, and bark, as I did for the forge blower (see page 186). But discovering new ways to work with natural materials is what I enjoy the most about primitive technology. I love borrowing from the world around me to create something useful.

I hope primitive technology inspires you as much as it did me to engage with the outdoors. Thanks for watching and reading.

BASIC
TOOL
KIT

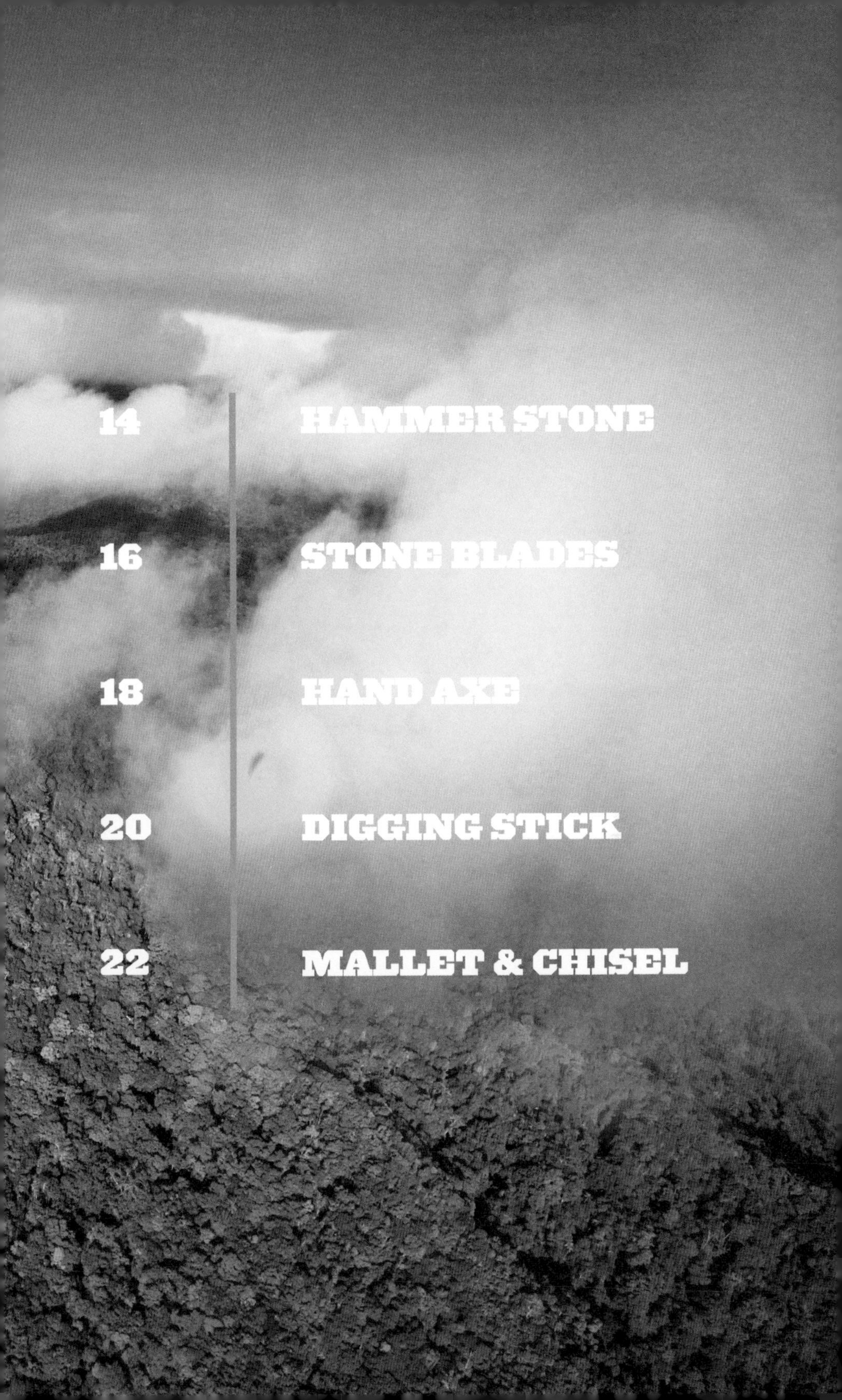

14   **HAMMER STONE**

16   **STONE BLADES**

18   **HAND AXE**

20   **DIGGING STICK**

22   **MALLET & CHISEL**

HAMMER STONE

The hammer stone is used for shaping other stones into usable tools. Because this tough stone tool is so simple to make, prehuman primates used it to shape their implements before metals became the primary materials for contouring. You'll have a sense of the hammer stone's origins if you watch a monkey crack open nuts with a stone.

The hammer stone is a core part of your primitive toolbox; fortunately, it is one of the easiest tools to make. All you need is two hard stones: one will be your hammer stone and the other will be used to shape it.

MATERIALS

1 hard stone (to be made into your hammer stone)

1 hard stone for hammering

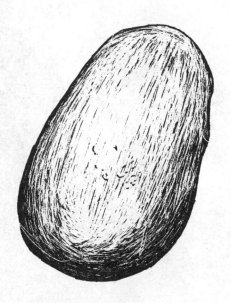

1. Determine the size of your hammer stone. The ideal size of stones used for shaping tools is usually between a golf ball and a tennis ball. But if you intend to pound boulders into shape or hammer wooden stakes into the ground, you will require a larger hammer stone that needs to be wielded with two hands.

2. To shape the cutting edge of your hammer stone, hold the stone that is being made into your tool in your nondominant hand. Hold the hard stone for hammering in your dominant hand. Brace it on the ground to strike it.

3. With the hard stone for hammering, strike the very edge of the stone that is being made into your tool at an angle so that a small flake is removed. Stone is removed from the opposite side of the edge you are striking, so never strike the side that is flaking. Be sure to strike the stone at an angle; the energy of perpendicular strikes is absorbed by the stone and can cause catastrophic breakage. Continue striking the stone until you have achieved the desired cutting edge for your hammer stone.

TIP

Quartz is the hardest and toughest stone, so it makes the best hammer stones. If quartz isn't available, choose a stone that is at least as strong as the stone you are shaping. Avoid using soft stones like chalk or gypsum.

USEFUL HAMMERING TECHNIQUES

Knapping: Make small strikes with your hammer stone in a downward motion near the edge of the stone you are shaping to remove little flakes. Keep the strikes small to avoid removing too much of the stone.

Pecking: Create a more deliberate edge for the stone you are shaping by making small strikes with your hammer stone to form tiny craters in the surface near the edge of the stone. Then grind this uneven, pockmarked finish against a rough stone to smooth out the edge.

STONE BLADES

Simple to make, stone blades are multipurpose staples in a primitive technician's tool kit. Use them for fine cutting and carving work or as knives, scrapers, and awls. Keep a pile of different sizes on hand; the more variety the better. A good way to develop a diverse collection is to save the stone scraps you accumulate from other projects (such as the flakes from the hammer stone you just made) and sharpen them as needed.

TOOLS AND MATERIALS

Scraps from a durable stone (quartz, flint, or obsidian is best)

Hammer Stone (page 14)

Hold the stone scrap in your nondominant hand and make small strikes with the hammer stone in a downward motion to chip small shards off the scrap. Continue chipping until you have achieved the desired shape for your blade.

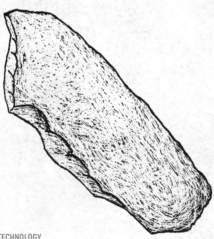

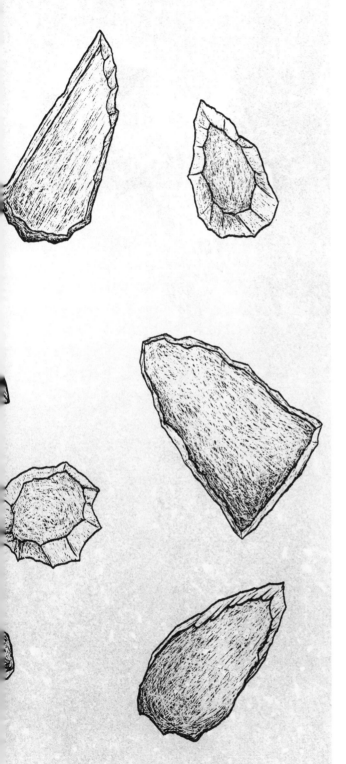

TIPS

➤ Follow the direction of the stone's natural shape rather than try to create a new shape.

➤ Chip the edges of a dull blade to reveal a new sharp edge.

➤ Sharpen long, pointed stones into awls; fashion small chips into all-purpose cutting blades. For heavy-duty tasks, sharpen the edge of a long, flat rock to use as a saw or a carpentry plane.

HOW TO USE A STONE BLADE

To carve wood, hold the blade against the wood and press down with your thumb on the blunt side to make a notch. Be sure to use a stone blade that is sharp on only one side. To drill wood, twist a pointed stone blade into the wood. Use a larger stone blade to plane the wood, removing rough edges with a scraping motion.

HAND AXE

The hand axe was the first stone cutting tool I developed; it is best used for light woodcutting tasks rather than large-scale logging. I have used a hand axe to construct structures from logs 6 inches (15 cm) thick, but it's hard on your hands, so I don't recommend it (use the Celt Axe, page 94, instead).

Choose a tough, durable stone for your axe blade. I often use basalt, which is common, but flint and obsidian are also good options.

TOOLS AND MATERIALS

1 durable stone
(for the axe blade)

Hammer Stone (page 14)

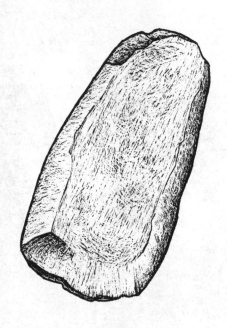

1. Hold the durable stone in your nondominant hand and determine which side is more blunt. The sharper edge will be your blade for cutting; the blunt edge will be used as a handle.

2. Strike the edge of the sharp side of the stone with the hammer stone in a downward motion while bracing it against the ground. Flip the stone over and repeat this process on the other side of the blade so that the edge stays roughly straight. The blade will start to look wavy if too much stone is removed from one side; in that case, even it out by flipping the stone over and striking from the other side.

3. To smooth the handle side of the blade, lightly tap downward on any protruding edges with the hammer stone.

HOW TO USE A HAND AXE

To remove wedges of timber from a tree, hold the axe in your dominant hand and swing it toward the tree at an angle. Keep your hand slightly relaxed in order to lessen the impact of each strike. Use a hand axe to cut small trees or saplings about 2 inches (5 cm) thick (use a Celt Axe, page 94, to cut larger trees).

DIGGING STICK

HOW TO USE A DIGGING STICK

Kneel on the ground and use a stabbing or scraping motion with your digging stick to excavate the soil. The technique should feel like paddling a canoe. If you encounter big roots, use a hand axe to chop them into manageable pieces, then use the digging stick as a lever to pull up the roots and break them. Use a digging stick to scoop out soil or clay, dig a hole for a fire pit, make mud or pottery, or till soil for gardening.

TIP

Digging is much harder if the soil is dry. To make the process easier, wet the area of the ground where you're planning to dig before you start.

A digging stick is much easier to make than a typical shovel, but it works just as well. Whenever I build huts or furnaces from mud, I use a digging stick to dig up the soil and mix it with water. It can also be used for gardening or harvesting root vegetables.

TOOLS AND MATERIALS

1 small branch or sapling, about 1.5 inches (4 cm) wide (the type of wood doesn't matter as long as it's durable)

Hand Axe (page 18)

Fire (see page 33) or Stone Blade (page 16)

1 sharp rock (if using fire)

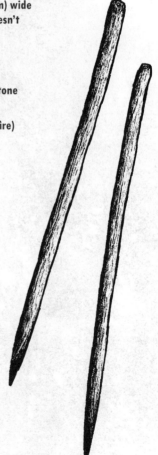

1. Hold the branch or sapling with your nondominant hand and use the hand axe to cut off a length that's about 2.5 feet long.

2. Start a fire. Burn the tip of the stick until it's charred (A); then scrape the char off onto a sharp rock until the tip becomes a sharp, hard point (B). Charring the tip of the stick will make it harder and more durable over the long term, but be careful not to burn away too much wood. If you aren't able to make a fire, use a stone blade to scrape off the bark and then sharpen the digging end to a point.

MALLET & CHISEL

I used a mallet and chisel for the first time when I began making Celt axes; they worked exceptionally well for carving the holes the axe head fit into on the handle. I also use a mallet and chisel to make the small, fine, precise cuts needed for carpentry joints.

TOOLS AND MATERIALS

Hammer Stone (page 14)

1 elongated piece of basalt or granite, about 6.5 inches (16.5 cm) long (for the chisel blade; fallen deer antlers will work too)

1 rough durable stone (for grinding and smoothing the chisel; basalt or sandstone is a good choice)

Hand Axe (page 18)

1 piece of timber, about 12 inches (30.5 cm) long and about 3 inches (7.5 cm) thick (for the mallet)

Water for polishing stone

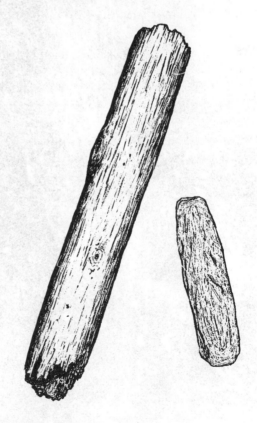

1. To make the chisel, use the hammer stone to shape one end of the basalt or granite stone into a rough cutting edge.

2. Wet the rough stone and grind the cutting edge of the chisel against it until the edge is neat and sharp.

3. Use the hammer stone to blunt the opposite end of the chisel (the end that will be struck with the mallet) and grind it against the rough stone until it is as flat as possible. It's important to remove any sharp edges from the top of the chisel so that it won't damage the mallet upon striking.

4. To make the mallet, use the hand axe or chisel to remove any excess wood from the end of the timber. Tapering the end of the mallet will make it more comfortable to use.

HOW TO USE A MALLET AND CHISEL

Hold the chisel in one hand at an angle against the piece of wood to be carved. Use the mallet to strike the blunt end of the chisel. The blade will bite into the surface and remove small chips of wood.

HOW TO GARDEN

The best way to cultivate a reliable food source is through gardening. Creating a garden may seem daunting, but it's actually just as simple as hunting or building a tool (sometimes it's even easier).

The most important part of any successful garden is its location. Take advantage of all the natural resources available to you. For example, do you have access to a water source such as a pond or a lake? If you do, then position your garden as close to that water source as possible, especially if rain is sparse or the land is particularly dry. Crops should have access to plenty of sunlight. Six hours a day is optimal, though certain plants can get by with less exposure.

Digging Stick (page 20)

Celt Axe (page 94) or Adze (page 90)

4 pieces of timber, each about 3 feet (1 m) long (for the fence posts)

1 pot or finely woven basket (for carrying water and/or leaf mulch to fertilize crops)

Tubers or seedlings

Water

Hammer Stone (page 14)

Flexible saplings or cane at least 3 feet (1 m) long, preferably longer (for enclosing the fence). Collect as needed.

Leaf mulch and wood ash to increase fertility

1. Use the digging stick to mark off a patch of land intended for cultivation. Use Celt axes or adzes to clear the land and cut the wood for the fence posts. The size of the plot depends on how much you want to grow. An area 10 feet (3 m) square will be a good start that can be enlarged later.

2. Dig up the soil with the digging stick, form into mounds, and mix in leaf mulch to improve soil tilth. Add wood ash from the fire to boost fertility.

3. Plant tubers or seedlings in the mounds. Sweet potatoes are a good choice: they provide the greatest food value per space and time of any crop. Water your crops.

4. Space the fence posts about 10 inches (25 cm) apart around the perimeter of the garden, and use the hammer stone to pound them into the ground.

5. Weave flexible saplings or cane in and out between the posts to enclose the fence.

HOW TO GROW YAMS

Yams are one of the most useful plants you can grow for food. They're versatile and pretty easy to cultivate. The plants grow both underground and on long climbing vines that can be wrapped around stakes or small saplings if your garden area is heavily forested.

1. Use a hammer stone to pound an odd number of wooden stakes into the ground to form an enclosure 1.5 to 3 feet (0.5 to 1 m) in diameter. It has to be an odd number or the weaving material will not alternate between the stakes correctly.

2. Weave cane or flexible saplings in and out through the stakes to form a basket that will keep your crops safe from animals.

3. Plant a yam tuber in the enclosure and cover with leaf litter; water.

4. Use the hammer stone to pound 3 10-feet (3 m) stakes into the ground for the vines to climb up.

5. After six months of growth, a large tuber will be ready to dig up. Harvest it with a digging stick and save the top of the yam to replant for next season.

TIP

Yams are cooked much like potatoes. They can be roasted in a fire pit, steamed, cut into chips and baked, mashed, or dried and pulverized into a flour to be used later in cooking.

HEAT

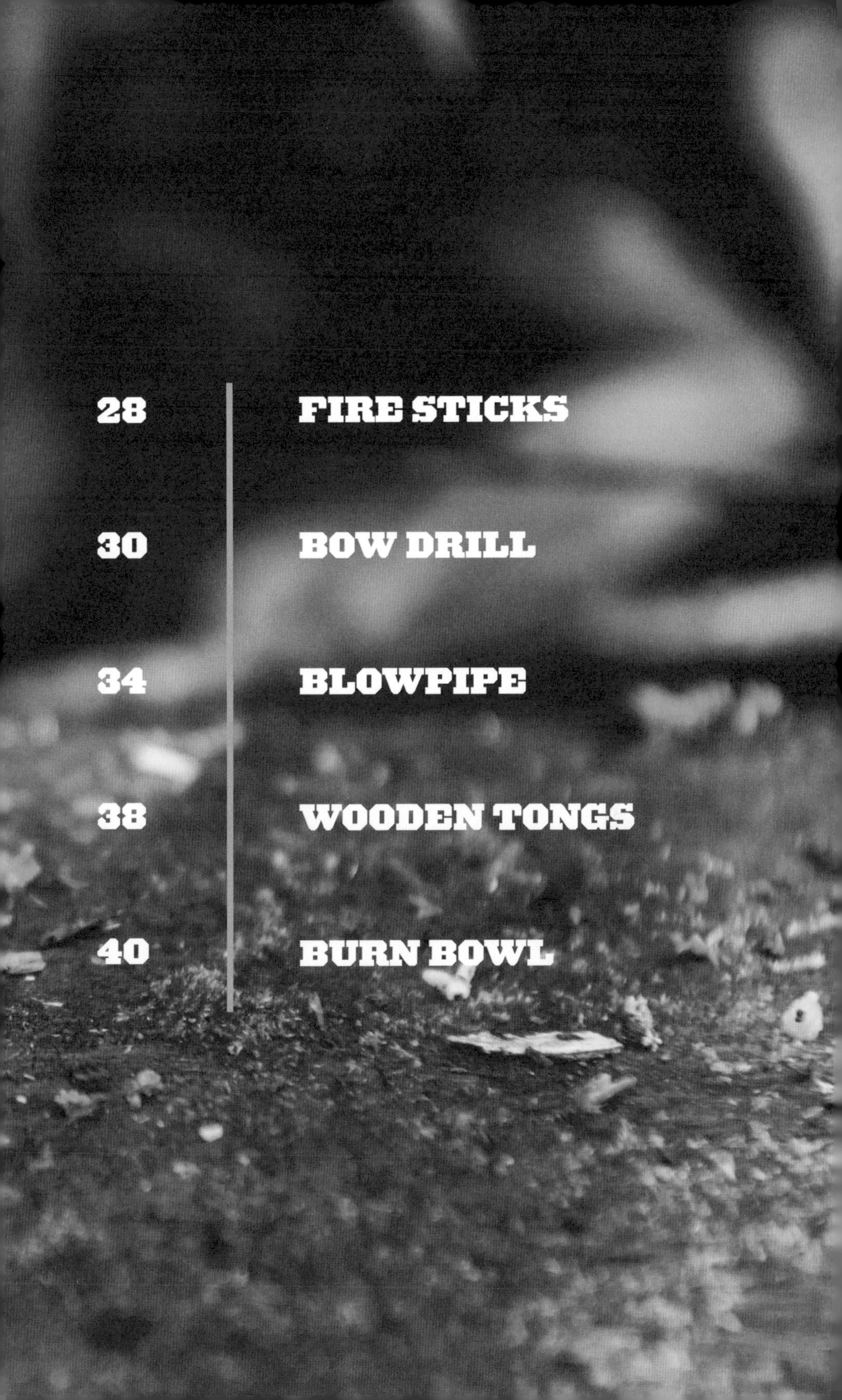

28   **FIRE STICKS**

30   **BOW DRILL**

34   **BLOWPIPE**

38   **WOODEN TONGS**

40   **BURN BOWL**

FIRE STICKS

Most methods of making fire are variations on this tool, which is similar in construction to the hand drill, a stick spun between the hands with the lower end drilling into something. Using fire sticks instead of glass or steel wool is an easier way to start a fire, but repetition and skill are required to master the technique. I practiced for weeks before being able to start a fire on the first try, but now it's a routine part of a typical day in the bush.

TOOLS AND MATERIALS

Hand Axe (page 18)

1 thin shoot from a tree or a bush, at least 23.5 inches (60 cm) long about ⅓ inch (1 cm) thick (for the spindle)

1 thick piece of wood, such as a plank-like piece of timber, at least 23.5 inches (60 cm) long (for the baseboard)

Stone Blade (page 16)

Fibrous material, such as leaf skeletons, crushed bark fiber, fibrous fungus, or palm fiber (for the tinder bundle)

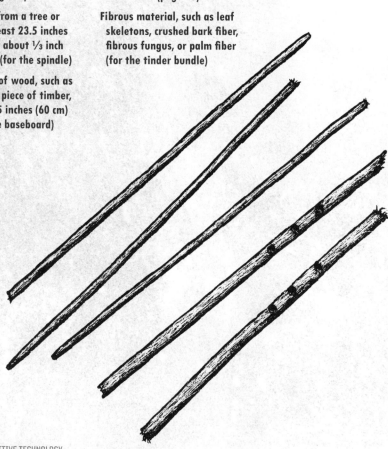

1. Use the hand axe to cut wood for the spindle and baseboard. Use the stone blade to scrape the bark off the thin wood shoot that will be your spindle and the thicker plank that will be your baseboard. This will help the sticks to dry faster. If the fire sticks are still green, leave them in a sunny spot to dry out or dry them near a fire (if you have one already made).

2. Use the stone blade to carve a small hole (a socket) in the baseboard big enough to fit the end of the spindle (A).

3. Use the stone blade to carve a notch below the socket along the side of the baseboard; hot powder will spill out from here once your fire gets going.

4. Use the stone blade to abrade the tip of the thicker end of the spindle so that it has a sharp point. The point should fit comfortably into the baseboard socket (B).

5. Crush the leaves and bark for the tinder bundle so that the fibers separate (C). If the fibers are too green or not dry enough, leave them out in the sun until they're crunchy.

BOW DRILL

HOW TO USE A BOW DRILL

Wrap the cord of the bow around the spindle and place the lower end of the spindle into the baseboard (for starting a fire) or the object to be drilled if making holes. Fit the indentation of the socket to the top of the spindle and hold it steady with your nondominant hand. Hold the bow with your other hand and draw it back and forth to rotate the spindle; do this rapidly to make a fire.

Use a bow drill to start a fire or to drill holes that can't be made by hand. For simplicity's sake, I prefer to use a hand drill, but a bow drill is a good alternative if you find it difficult to start a fire with a hand drill.

TOOLS AND MATERIALS

Stone Blade (page 16)

1 piece of wood, shell, or bone that fits easily in the hand (for the socket or drill piece)

Hand Axe (page 18)

1 thin shoot from a tree or a bush about 1 foot (30 cm) long and ¾ inch (2 cm) thick (for the spindle; it should be thicker and sturdier than the wood used to make the fire stick spindle)

Fibrous bark (for weaving into cordage; see page 76)

Flexible piece of wood, about 20 inches (50 cm) long (for the bow)

1. Use the stone blade to carve an indentation into the piece of wood, shell, or bone to make the socket that the end of the spindle will rest against.

2. Use the hand axe to cut wood for the spindle. Cut a spindle for the bow to spin. This should be thicker than a fire stick that is spun by hand so that it won't bend from sideways forces of the bow. Sharpen the ends of the spindle to fit into the socket and baseboard. Carve a notch in the socket of the baseboard for the powder to pour out of.

3. Make cordage from some fibrous bark.

4. Use the hand axe to cut the wood for the bow. Tie the cord to each end so that it forms a bow. It doesn't need to bend and can instead be a ridged curved stick. If you are using the bow drill to start a fire, the baseboard should be made from suitable timber (see page 28). The spindle and baseboard for this method can be made of denser timber than the hand drill.

HOW TO START A FIRE

1. Sit cross-legged on the ground, put the tinder bundle on the ground, and place the baseboard on top of it; use your foot to hold the baseboard in place. It's often helpful to put a small twig down flat between the baseboard and the tinder to help get the air moving between the wood and the powder.

2. Place the pointed end of the spindle in the socket of the baseboard and hold the spindle between the palms of your hands.

3. Rapidly spin the spindle between your hands while applying moderate downward force. Your hands will move down the stick as you do this, so when you reach the bottom, stop and quickly start at the top of the spindle again. Use speed rather than force to avoid blisters.

4. Soon smoke will appear from the powder pouring out of the socket, which will change from brown to black, indicating it is beginning to char from the heat. Don't stop drilling until you see the pile of powder begin to smoke by itself.

5. When the powder starts to smoke, lift up the tinder bundle and gently blow on the coal so it glows red and ignites the tinder.

6. When a large portion of the tinder has ignited, put it into the fire pit and cover it with thin sticks for kindling.

7. Blow on the tinder until the kindling catches, then add larger pieces of wood to stoke the fire.

BLOWPIPE

A blowpipe is a tube used to blow air into a fire to make it hotter. It is useful for stoking a coal into flames, which makes starting a fire easier, or for shaping wood with fire, which can produce cleaner mortises in wood or indentations for a burn trough or bowl than carving or drilling.

TOOLS AND MATERIALS

1 hollow stem (bamboo is preferable, but if it's not available use a fast-growing stem with a soft core)

Digging Stick (page 20)

Stone Blade (page 16)

Clay for coating the end of the pipe

A thin stick (about ¼ inch [5 mm] thick) to make a hole in the clay

1. If the stem is not hollow already, use a digging stick to dig out the soft core pith (A).

2. Use the stone blade to cut the hollow stem to a reasonable length (B) to keep the user's mouth from the heat of the fire (at least 12 inches [30.5 cm]).

HOW TO USE A BLOWPIPE

1. To burn a hole in a piece of wood, carve the beginnings of one using a stone blade.

2. Place hot coals into the indentation just made using twigs so that they sit right next to the wood to be burnt.

3. Use the blowpipe to blow on the coals until they glow and start burning the wood. You'll probably need to do this more than once, so be careful not to breathe the flames back into the pipe.

4. Aim the air onto the wood to be burned rather than the coals; the coals provide excess heat to prevent the charring wood from going out. Stop blowing every so often and scrape out charred wood with a stone.

5. Coat other parts of the wood with wet clay to prevent them from burning.

WOODEN TONGS

TIP

When using tongs at high temperatures, it sometimes helps to coat your hands in wet clay to protect them from radiant heat. Over time the tongs will burn away, so it may be necessary to make multiple tongs.

HOW TO USE WOODEN TONGS

Holding the tongs at the lashed end, position the distal ends around the object to be lifted and then squeeze to clamp the arms of the tongs around it. Lift the object. To release, relax your grip on the tongs. If the object becomes wedged in the tongs, use force to open the tongs by pulling both arms of the tongs outward.

Tongs are used to manipulate materials in nature that are too hot or dangerous to hold in your hands. They're a convenient cooking tool for picking up hot coals, burning logs, or food fresh from the fire.

TOOLS AND MATERIALS

Hand Axe (page 18)

Wood that splits well, specifically any wood with a straight grain, such as pine, at least 20 inches (50 cm) long

Cordage (page 76) or vine for lashing the tongs together

1 small stone or wedge of wood (for holding the tongs open)

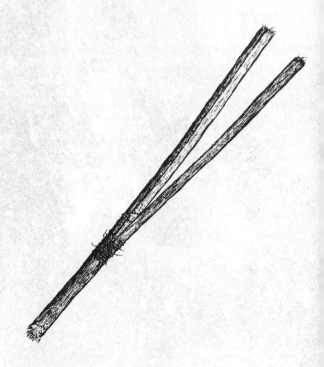

1. Use the hand axe to cut a piece of wood as long as the tongs are intended to be: at least 20 inches (50 cm) or longer if the tongs are to be used for reaching into deep furnaces (A).

2. Split the timber partially through with the hand axe. Use the cordage to lash the opposite end to prevent it from splitting all the way down the length of the wood (B).

3. Push the small stone or wedge of wood into the split down to the lashing to hold the tongs open (C).

BURN BOWL

A burn bowl is a wooden trough made by using fire to burn out a depression in the lump of wood. This technique is particularly useful when you need to create large indentations in wood.

TOOLS AND MATERIALS

Stone Blade (page 16)

1 chunk of wood (see Tip), as small as 10 inches (25 cm) and as large as 20 inches (50 cm) in diameter

Fire (see page 33)

Wooden Tongs (page 38) or sticks

Blowpipe (page 34)

Mud or clay

You can use any type of wood for this project. A dense wood will take longer to burn but will be durable; a less dense wood will burn quickly but may not be as sturdy.

Carefully tip out the coals after the wood has charred; use the stone blade to deepen the depression by scraping out the char. Repeat until the bowl is as deep as you want it to be. Rinse away any clay or mud before using the bowl.

1. Use the stone blade to carve the beginning of the depression in the lump of wood that will form the bowl (A).

2. Take hot coals from the fire using tongs or sticks and place the coals into the depression (B). Use the blowpipe to fan the flames, or simply blow on them or fan them with your hands. The idea is to get the wood underneath to start to burn by itself. To avoid burning the sides or other parts of the bowl, plaster the area to be protected with mud or clay (C).

3. Keep the coals on the burning wood after it starts to glow; removing them will cause the wood to cool down and stop burning.

HOW TO BOIL WATER USING A BURN BOWL

When you need to boil water for cooking or drinking but don't have access to a ceramic or fire-safe container, stone boiling is a great technique to use to heat water quickly.

1. Choose a handful of large, thick stones. Make sure that up to 2 at a time can fit in the bottom of the burn bowl.

2. Place the stones in a fire pit and start a fire (see page 33) on top of them.

3. While the stones are heating up, fill the burn bowl with water. Don't fill it all the way, as the stones will displace a lot of water when they are put in the bowl.

4. When the stones are glowing red-hot use wooden tongs to place them into the burn bowl.

The water should boil on the stones' submerged surfaces. When the temperature of the stones and water has equalized, remove the cold stones and add new hot ones.

5. After a few rounds of adding stones, the water should be at a rolling boil. If the water isn't boiling, heat the stones for longer periods of time before adding them to the bowl.

HUNT

46   BOW

50   FISH TRAP

54   SPEAR THROWER

58   SLING

BOW

Hunting is heavily restricted in Australia, but regulations differ from region to region. Familiarize yourself with the hunting laws in your area before you make and use a bow or any of the other weapons in this section.

TOOLS AND MATERIALS

Hand Axe (page 18)

Strong flexible timber 2 feet (125 cm) long and 2 inches (5 cm) thick (for the stave)

Mallet and Chisel (page 22)

Cordage (page 76) made from fibrous bark (for the string)

Thin shoots (for the arrows)

Fire (see page 33)

Stone Blade (page 16)

Feathers (for the arrow fletching)

Tree resin or thin strips of bark fiber

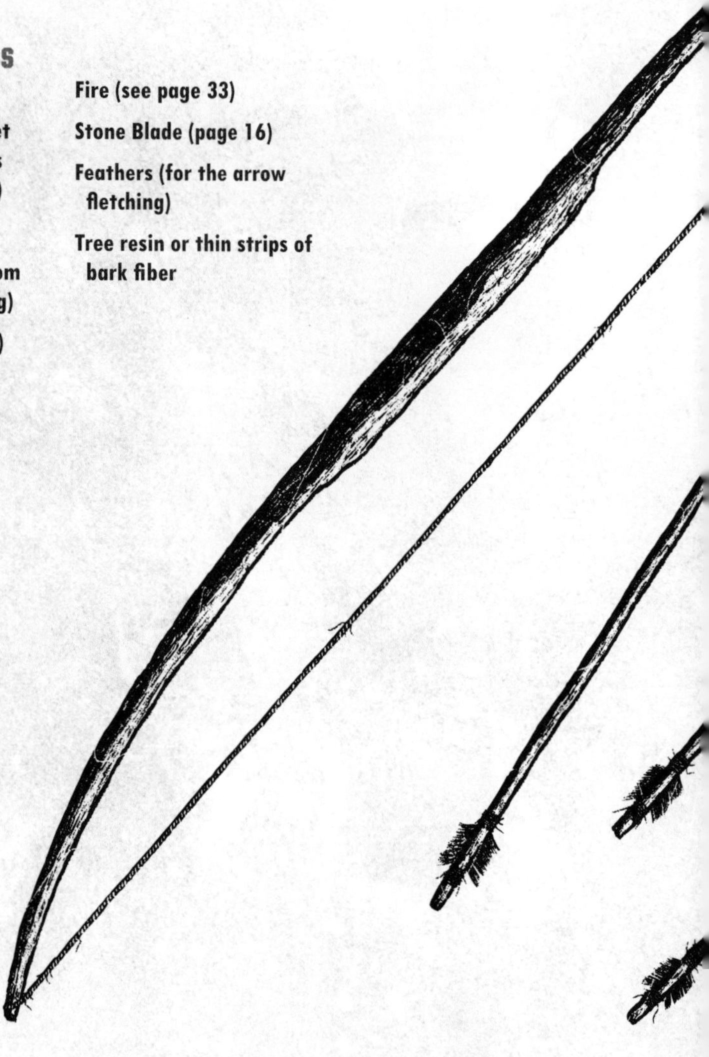

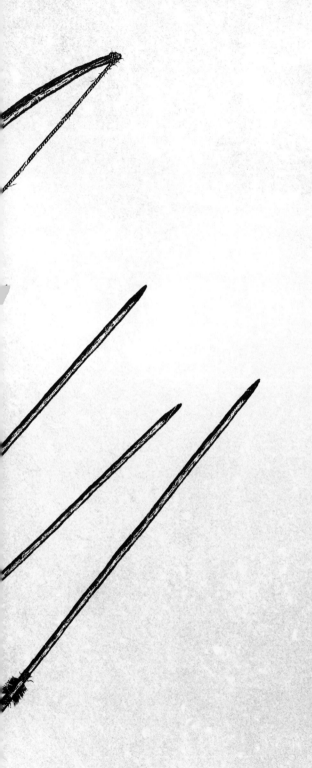

HOW TO USE
A BOW AND ARROW

Use one hand to hold the bow in the middle (most people use their left hand) and nock an arrow onto the string. Let the back end of the arrow rest on the hand holding the bow. Draw the string back and look down the arrow at the target. When the two are lined up, release the arrow.

1. To make the short bow, use the hand axe to cut wood for a stave about 4 feet (1.25 m) long (A).

2. Use the mallet and chisel to split the stave in half. If the stave twists, split off wood at the ends on opposite sides to remove the twist (B).

3. Use the hand axe to chop wood off the belly so that the stave tapers in thickness and width from the middle to the tips.

4. Use the chisel to cut notches in the tips of the stave for tying the string (C). Narrow the width of the handle at the middle of the bow using the chisel.

5. To make the string, collect strips of fibrous bark and twist it into a cord longer than the length of the bow. Tie the string onto the notches in the tips of the stave using half hitches (D).

6. To make the arrows, use the hand axe to cut thin shoots about 23.5 inches (60 cm) long and $\frac{1}{3}$ inch (1 cm) wide.

7. Sharpen the thicker end of the arrow by charring it in a fire and scraping the char off onto a rock (E).

8. Use the stone blade or chisel to carve a nock for the string into the back of the arrow about $\frac{1}{3}$ inch (1 cm) deep and $\frac{1}{5}$ inch (4 mm) wide.

9. Split the feathers and use the halves to form the flights for the arrows.

10. Use tree resin to glue the fletching onto the back end of the arrow, or tie the feathers down using thin strips of bark fiber. Use 2 or 3 flights per arrow (F).

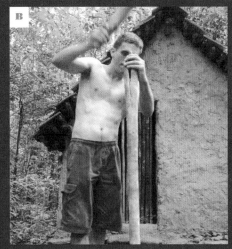

FISH TRAP

A fish trap consists of a large basket with a funnel at its opening. Fish swim into the funnel easily but cannot so easily find their way out due to the narrow opening being hard to access when swimming back the way they came.

TOOLS AND MATERIALS
Stone Blade (page 16)

Flexible vines, cane, or saplings (for weaving), cut as needed

9 20-inch (50 cm) long sticks (for the ribs of the basket and the cone)

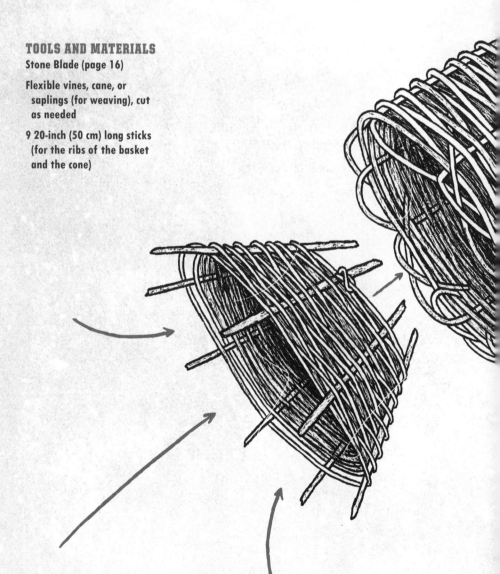

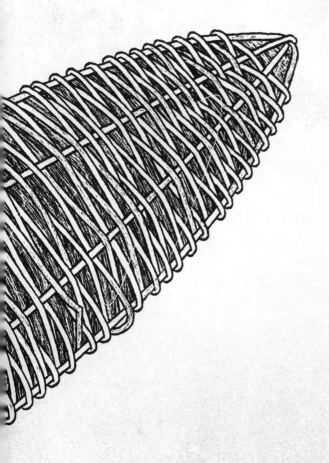

HOW TO CATCH A FISH WITH A FISH TRAP

Put the trap into a body of water known to contain fish. If you have bait, put it in the trap to entice fish, but it's not really necessary: inquisitive fish and aquatic animals will find their way into the trap simply because they investigate foreign objects that enter their waters. Check the trap after a few hours. Eat what you catch and use any leftover scraps as bait. Throw the trap back in the water and check it the next day.

1. Use the stone blade to cut the vines, cane, or saplings for the basket and the funnel (A). Use any of the techniques on pages 64, 68, and 72 to weave a basket at least 20 inches (50 cm) long.

2. To form the funnel, make a cone out of sticks and tie them together at one end with vine (B). Use an odd number of sticks to form the cone if you used the standard weaving technique to make the basket (even numbers cause the weaves to stack incorrectly, and the basket will have no tension).

3. Weave flexible materials between the ribs of the cone (C). Pull the sticks back so that an opening is formed in the narrow end of the cone. Assemble the trap by placing the funnel into the opening of the basket.

SPEAR THROWER

A spear thrower consists of a piece of wood with a spur in one end. It is a weapon that uses the lever principle to throw spears farther than is possible by hand alone. One butt of the spear has a cup-shaped depression to accommodate the spur. Because it is flexible, the spear stores energy during the throw, like a spring, so that it leaps off the end of the thrower with greater speed when it is released. The flexible spear wobbles during flight, but the oscillations stabilize its trajectory so that it won't tumble front over back.

TOOLS AND MATERIALS
Hand Axe (page 18) or Celt Axe (page 94)

Flexible saplings (use a sapling with a side branch growing outward for the thrower)

Fire (see page 33)

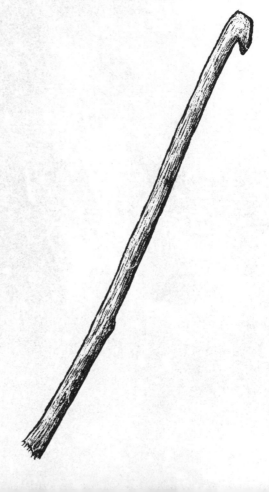

1. To make the thrower, use the hand axe or Celt axe to cut the sapling with a side branch. It should be cut just below the stem growing outward from the main stem (A).

2. Cut the stem growing outward short so that it forms a small spur. The thrower should be about 1.5 times the length of your forearm (B).

3. To make the spear, use the hand axe or Celt axe to cut a sapling that is ⅓ inch to ¾ inch (1 to 2 cm) thick. Start a fire and burn one end of the spear; sharpen it to a point by scraping the char off on a rock (C).

4. Use the hand axe to carve a cup-shaped depression into the butt of the spear that will accommodate the spur of the thrower.

HOW TO THROW A SPEAR WITH A SPEAR THROWER

Hold the spear thrower in your throwing hand and place the cup of the spear into the spur of the thrower. Use the last three fingers of your hand to hold the thrower and your thumb and index finger to hold the spear in place. To start the throw, whip the thrower straight forward. If done correctly, the spear should flex first, then spring off the spur of the thrower toward the target, not tumble front over back.

SLING

A sling consists of a pouch with two lengths of cord extending from opposite sides. It is a weapon used to throw stones farther than can be done by hand alone. A stone is placed in the pouch and it is swung over the head before being released toward the target. It's a bit difficult to master the technique, but the sling is easy to make and the ammunition can be found anywhere.

TOOLS AND MATERIALS

Hand Axe (page 18)

Fibrous material, such as the inner bark of trees (for Cordage, page 76)

Round stones or clay balls (for ammunition; fire the clay balls to make them harder if desired; see page 176)

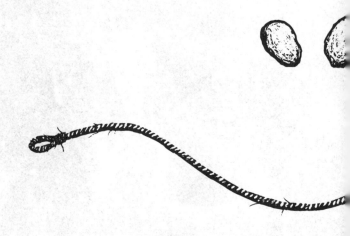

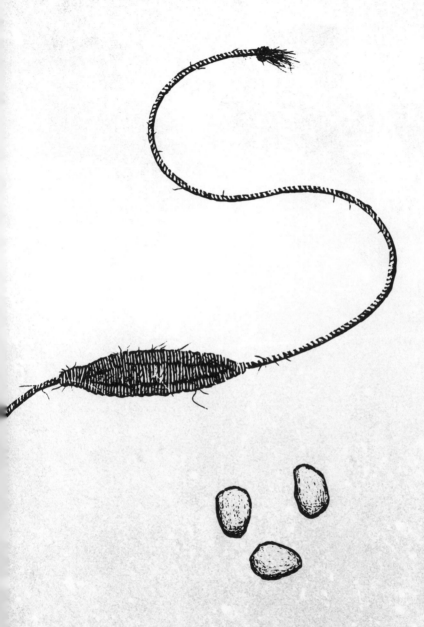

1. Use the hand axe to harvest the fibrous material; pull apart strips as long as your arm span and use them to make cordage (A).

2. Fold the cord over and tie 2 sheepshank knots in the middle of the cord so that 3 pieces form a central pouch. Weave finer strands of the same fibrous material over and under these 3 pieces of cord to form a woven pouch (B).

3. Tie a loop at one end of the cord to slip over the index finger of your throwing hand and a knot in the other end to hold with your thumb before releasing the sling (C).

HOW TO USE A SLING

→ Slip the loop at one end of the cord over the index finger of your throwing hand. Hold the knot at the other end of the sling with your thumb against the index finger of the throwing hand. Place a stone in the pouch of the sling.

→ With your other hand, hold the pouch forward toward the target; keep your throwing hand back. With the holding hand, toss the pouch over the shoulder of your holding hand. As it swings behind, bring your throwing hand forward in a coordinated throwing motion. Release the sling as it reaches 90 degrees to the target. The rock should fly forward toward the target. Accuracy will take a good deal of target practice.

CLOTHING
& TEXTILES

64 | **STANDARD WEAVE BASKET**

68 | **COIL WEAVE BASKET**

72 | **TWINING WEAVE BASKET**

76 | **CORDAGE**

78 | **DROP SPINDLE**

80 | **LOOM**

84 | **SANDALS**

STANDARD WEAVE BASKET

A basket is a container woven from flexible materials; it is used to carry or hold items that would otherwise be too cumbersome to cart by hand or too untidy to leave lying in a pile on the ground. Baskets can be made from a variety of materials, and are woven in different ways. The standard weave basket is made from flexible materials, such as cane, using a basic over-and-under weave. These simple baskets were the first ones I learned to make. I've used them for years to carry and store tools and materials, especially large quantities of charcoal.

TOOLS AND MATERIALS
Stone Blade (page 16)

Flexible cane, saplings, or vines resistant to splintering when bent, cut as needed

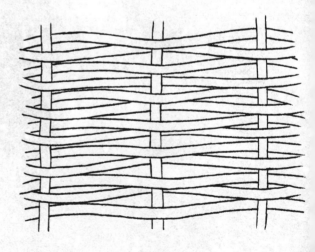

1. Use the stone blade to cut 4 lengths of cane about 5 feet (1.5 m) long. Lay them out so that they resemble the spokes of a wheel and cross in the center (A).

2. Cut another length of cane about 2.5 feet (75 cm) long, and add it to the circle (B).

3. Lash the spokes together at the center with some vine so that they stay together during the weaving process. Take another long length of cane and, starting at the center, weave over and under the spokes. When you come to the end of one length of cane, just pick up where you left off with a new one (C).

4. At this stage the basket is flat. When the flat bottom is as wide as is needed (say, 20 inches [50 cm]), sharply kink the spokes upward at a right angle and continue weaving (D). When the basket is as tall as you want it to be, bend each spoke and tuck it into the gap made by the adjacent spoke to prevent the loops of cane from sliding off the top of the basket and to form handles.

COIL WEAVE BASKET

HOW TO USE A COIL WEAVE BASKET

Use a coil weave basket to carry small items like seeds that would fall through a basket with a looser weave. If woven tightly enough, a coil weave basket can be used for carrying water.

When flexible cane is unavailable, make this basket from long coils of fibrous material. Long continuous spirals of thick coil are tied together using a thin thread-like material. Coil weave baskets can be made from two different materials: for example, I have made the coils from long grass and lashed them together with bark fiber strips. They're more time-consuming to make than standard weave baskets but are so neat and tightly woven that they can hold small grains or sometimes even water.

TOOLS AND MATERIALS

Stone Blade (page 16)

Fibrous material, such as long grass (for the coils)

Bark fiber, long grass, or pine needles (for lashing)

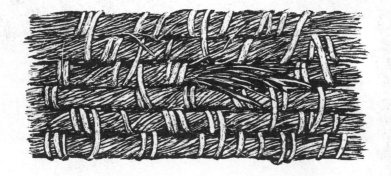

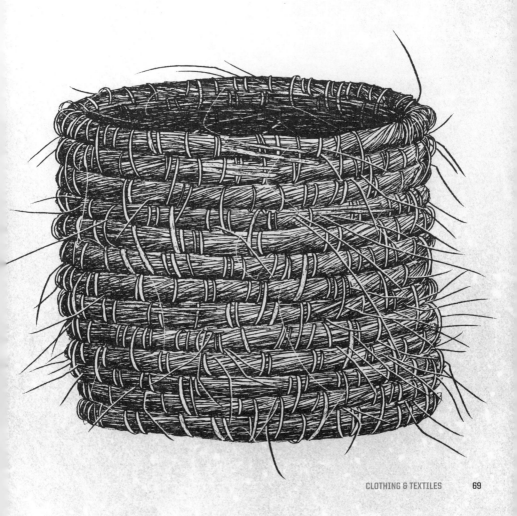

1. Use the stone blade to cut the fibrous material for the coils. Gather together a bunch of the coil material about the thickness of your thumb (A). Wrap the lashing material down the length of the coil material. The coil material forms the bulk of the basket and can be stiff, but the material used to lash the coils together needs to be flexible like string.

2. Start coiling the end of the bundle into a spiral. As you go, thread the lashing material through the previous coil (B).

3. Do 2 wraps of lashing material through the coil and then 1 wrap through the previous coil to attach the current. This is what prevents the coil from unraveling. Repeat the process: 2 wraps, 1 tie (C). As you run out of the coil material, just add new lengths.

4. When you come to the end of the lashing material, tie it to the coil and then tie on a new length. Shape the coils upward as you go; if you leave them flat, you'll be weaving a circular mat instead of a basket.

5. When the basket is as big as you want it to be, stop adding coil material and tie off the lashing material (D).

TWINING WEAVE BASKET

Of the three types of baskets in this section, the twining weave is probably the quickest to make. Two leading strands of material are twisted around the ribs of this basket in such a way that they form a long cord that spirals up the length of the basket. It doesn't matter how far apart each rib is because the twist rather than tension against the ribs holds the basket together. This technique is also useful for making fish traps in a hurry.

TOOLS AND MATERIALS

Stone Blade (page 16)

Stiff material, such as thin stems (for basket ribs)

Pliable material that can be twisted into shape, such as cane, vine, or bark strips (for twining)

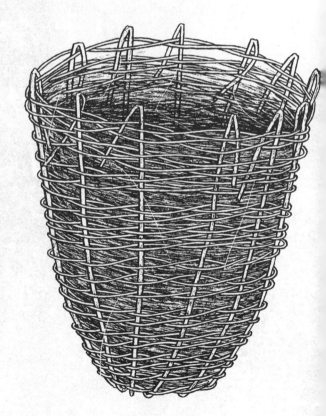

1. Use the stone blade to cut the stiff and pliable materials. To make the rough shape of the basket, gather the stiff material for the ribs at one end and lash them together with a pliable material (A). It doesn't matter if there are an even or odd number of ribs with this method.

2. Twist 2 strands of pliable material around each rib. Form the 2 leading ends into 1 twist between each rib before you move on to the next rib (B). This way, the two strands will form cord that contains each rib between its twist with each row.

3. Keep weaving around in this fashion until the basket is as big as you want it to be (C). Tie off the end with a granny knot.

CORDAGE

Tying things together is the most obvious use for cordage. It can also function as the string in a bow, a bow drill, a cord drill, and a pump drill, or as cords in a sling.

Cordage is created when two or more strands of fiber are twisted together in such a way that they will not unravel. Each of the two strands is twisted in one direction (e.g., clockwise), and the individual strands are twisted together in the opposite direction (counterclockwise). The unraveling forces cancel each other out, so the cordage stays intact. Use cordage to tie things together or as the string in a bow; you can knot it as you would ordinary rope.

TOOLS AND MATERIALS
Fibrous material, such as bark or animal sinews

1. Harvest the bark strips from a tree by cutting them off with a hand axe. Separate them into thin strips (A) and allow them to dry until they can be easily handled.

2. Take 2 strands of fiber and hold them together in one hand. With the other hand, twist the individual strands in one direction and then twist the 2 strands together in the opposite direction (B).

3. Add new fibers to the end of the strands until the cordage is as long as you want it to be: just remember to keep the thickness consistent (C).

DROP SPINDLE

HOW TO MAKE YARN WITH A DROP SPINDLE

Yarn is simply a single strand of twisted fiber. The strand stays together only because of the bite of the twisted fibers holding them. Parallel fibers that aren't twisted together will come apart; twisting them makes them hold tight. Yarn is not as strong as cordage, which is made up of at least two strands.

1. Twist a strand of fiber by hand and then tie it onto the fiber hook (small twig tied to the top) of the drop spindle.

2. Spin the drop spindle so that it begins twisting the fiber. Add more fibers as the strand runs out, but be sure to keep the yarn an even thickness.

A drop spindle is one of the easiest tools for making yarn that can then be woven into cloth. In my early years as a primitive technician, I tried weaving with cordage, but it was a long, messy process. Yarn is the best choice for weaving cloth.

TOOLS AND MATERIALS
Clay

1 stick, 6 to 12 inches (15.25 to 30.5 cm) long (for the spindle)

1 small twig (for the fiber hook)

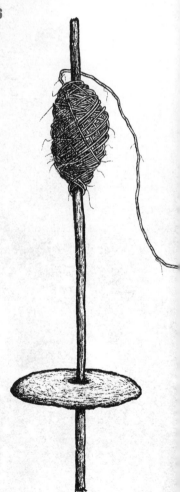

1. Wrap the clay around the stick and let it dry. This could be in the shape of a disk or a sphere so it acts like a flywheel when spun (A).

2. Using a small piece of fiber, such as that which is to be spun with the drop spindle, tie the small twig to the top of the stick to act as a hook to catch the strands of fiber to make them twist (B).

LOOM

A loom is a frame for weaving. I started using looms when I found out how difficult it is to weave cloth by hand.

TOOLS AND MATERIALS

Hammer Stone (page 14)

4 short sticks 25 cm long (for wooden pegs)

Thread or pieces of yarn (see page 78)

2 pieces of wood (for the stationary and movable crossbars) 2.5 feet (75 cm) long for a loom this wide

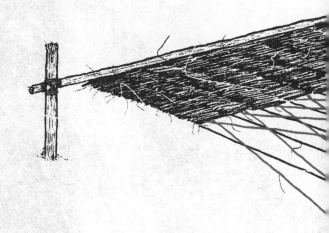

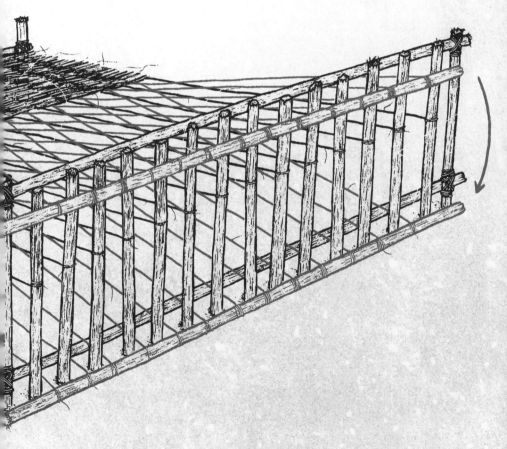

1. Use the hammer stone to hammer 2 pegs into the ground at one end of what will be the loom (A).

2. Have a stationary crossbar at one end of the loom tied to two stakes (B).

3. At the other end, at a distance that will be the length of the loom, hammer in half the number of pegs as there will be vertical threads. Space the threads according to how fine you want the cloth. For coarse fiber, 1 inch (2.5 cm) or more apart will do (any closer might be too tight).

4. Put the movable crossbar behind these pegs.

5. Tie the ends of the vertical threads to the stationary crossbar at one end. Tie the other ends of every first thread to a peg, and the other ends of every second thread, to the movable crossbar (C).

HOW TO MAKE CLOTH WITH A LOOM

With the moveable crossbar down, take a long spool of yarn and thread yarn through the gap between every first and second thread. This threads the yarn over and under the vertical threads.

Now, lift the crossbar, creating a new gap, and thread the yarn back through the threads in the opposite direction. This threads the yarn under and over the vertical threads, the opposite of when the cross bar was in the down position. This holds the cloth together.

When a square or rectangular piece of cloth is the size you want it to be, tie off the ends and take it off the loom.

SANDALS

This simple form of footwear covers only the soles of the feet; the sandals are held in place by cords tied through the toes. I first made these sandals when my feet began to get too damaged from walking barefoot all the time. They are particularly useful when you need to traverse rough terrain while carrying heavy loads. I still prefer to go barefoot, though.

TOOLS AND MATERIALS
Stone Blade (page 16)

Ropelike material that can be woven, such as lawyer cane, vines, or Cordage (page 76) made from long grass or bark fiber

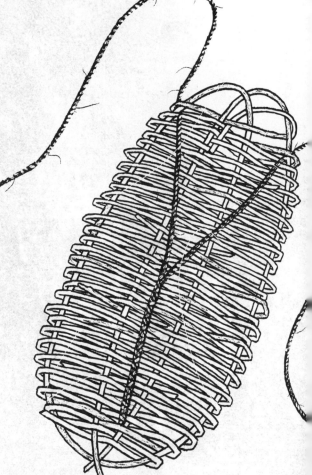

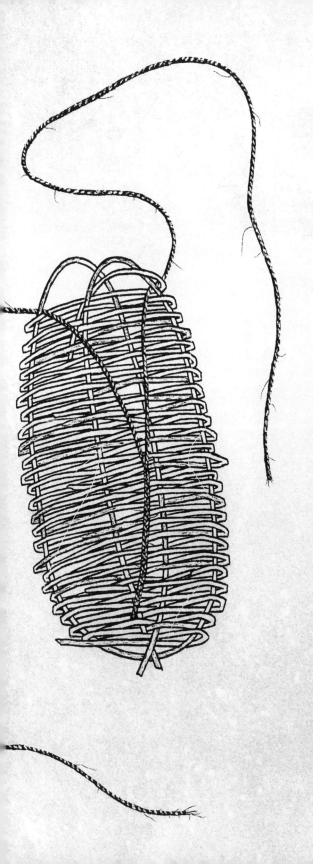

HOW TO WEAR YOUR SANDALS

Put the sandal on with the cord between the first and second toes.

TIP

Sandals woven from bark fiber are known as 5-mile shoes because they wear out quickly. Make multiple pairs so you always have a few on hand for when you need them.

1. Use the stone blade to cut a length of cane 6 times the length of the foot. Form it into 2 loops and hold them over the big toes to keep them in place while weaving (A).

2. There will be 4 strands to weave between. Start weaving the material over and under the 4 strands. Add new lengths as the old ones are used up (B).

3. When the weaving is finished, make some cordage and thread it through the area on the sole where the first and second toes will sit.

4. Braid these 2 ends together; they will form the rope that goes between the toes. Then split the cord again where the braid meets the top of the foot and thread it through the heel of the sole on both sides (C).

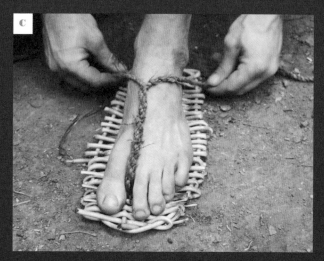

ADVANCED TOOL KIT

90   ADZE

94   CELT AXE

98   CORD DRILL

104   WATER HAMMER

ADZE

The stone adze (pronounced "ads") is an all-purpose woodworking tool consisting of a stone blade attached to an L-shaped handle. Although stone Celt axes are more durable, adzes are much easier to make because you don't have to worry as much about ensuring that the handle doesn't split during the manufacturing process.

TOOLS AND MATERIALS

Hammer Stone (page 14)

1 durable stone, such as basalt or granite (for the adze head)

1 large rough stone (for polishing the adze head)

Water

1 L-shaped piece of wood about 20 inches (50 cm) long (for the adze handle)

Hand Axe (page 18)

Lashing material, such as Cordage (page 76) or loya cane

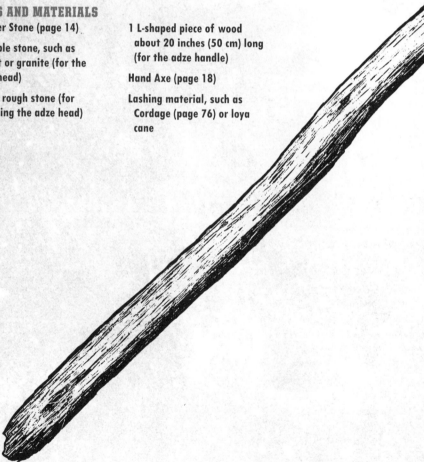

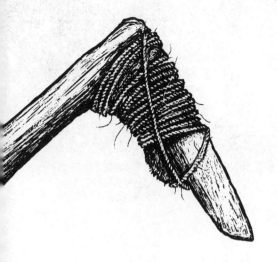

HOW TO USE AN ADZE

Hold the adze with both hands and swing it so that the head strikes the timber with the cutting edge. When felling trees, start with the adze over your shoulder and swing it forward. Cut around the tree until it falls. Once the tree is down, use the adze to plane the timber into planks or gouge wood out of the trunk to form it into a trough.

1. To make the adze head, use the hammer stone to hammer the durable stone into a rough shape by using the knapping technique (see page 14). Then use the pecking technique (see page 14) to refine the shape by removing any "hills and valleys" that may be left over from the knapping process (A).

2. Grind the adze head on a large rough stone to polish the edge (B). Wet the stone as you grind it; this helps the fine particles polish and smooth the surface.

3. To make the adze handle, select a piece of wood that has a right angle in it. This may be a tree that has fallen over and sprouted an L-shaped shoot. Use the hand axe to cut the handle and shape it so that it has a flat top (C).

4. Fit the adze head into the flat space on top of the handle so that the cutting edge protrudes by about 2 inches (5 cm), and secure them together using the lashing material: wrap the lashing material around the length of the head that is on the handle and slip the last ends under the previous loop (D).

CELT AXE

It took me a long time to perfect the Celt axe, one of the most durable tools I've made. While some axes rely on lashing material to hold them together, the Celt axe is designed to get stronger with use. With each strike, the axe head is wedged more tightly into the handle, preventing it from falling out. Once I figured out how to attach a durable handle that wouldn't split, it became my most efficient cutting tool.

TOOLS AND MATERIALS

Hammer Stone (page 14)

1 durable stone, such as
    basalt, granite, or limestone
    (for the axe head; see Tip)

1 grinding stone

Water

Hand Axe (page 18)

1 piece of timber, about
    12 inches (30.5 cm) long (for
    the axe handle; see Tip)

Mallet and Chisel (page 22)

TIPS

When choosing timber for your axe handle, aim for a type of wood that doesn't split easily. Wood that twists as it grows is a good choice, such as northern olive or wattle.

When choosing the stone for your axe head, try to pick one that's close to the shape of an axe head: a flat stone about twice as long as it is wide, tapering from front to back. The profile should be roughly triangular so that it will insert into the mortise; if it's not this shape already, then use the hammer stone to shape it.

Use the Celt axe much as you would a conventional axe, but cut closer to 90 degrees to the timber, because the stone head will be blunter than a metal blade.

1. To make the axe head, use the hammer stone to knap and peck (see page 14) the cutting edge of the durable stone.

2. Use the grinding stone and water to grind and polish the cutting edge of the blade until it is smooth (A).

3. To make the axe handle, use the hand axe to cut the timber to the required length. For a small hatchet, make it 19 to 20 inches (49 to 50 cm), or roughly the length from your elbow to the tip of your fingers. For a longer, heavier axe, make it about the height of your hip from the ground.

4. Use the mallet and chisel to carve a hole in the top end of the handle that goes through to the other side (B). If possible, position it between 2 knots in the wood; this will prevent splitting. If you're having trouble cutting all the way through from one side, cut from the other side and meet in the middle.

5. Insert the axe head into the hole (C). Only the top and bottom of the head should touch the mortise. If it touches either side, it's more likely that the handle will split because the wood grain runs vertically, meaning that the lateral outward force of the head can split the wood. Make a few practice chops before you shape the handle in case the wood splits and you need to start over.

6. Taper the handle to make it more ergonomic: a thicker handle would be harder to grip than a thinner one (D).

CORD DRILL

HOW TO USE A CORD DRILL

Wind the two ends of the cord around the spindle in the same direction. Place the sharpened end of the spindle onto the object to be drilled. Hold the ends of the cords in each hand and pull outward. The spindle will begin to spin as the cords unravel. The momentum will cause the cords to wrap back around the spindle in the other direction. Once the cords are wound back up, pull them back out again, repeating the process. The drill will spin rapidly in both directions. To drill a hole in the object, attach a stone bit to the lower end of the spindle. You can also use the cord drill as you would a fire stick to make fire.

A cord drill consists of a spindle with a flywheel attached to it; the middle of a cord is attached to the top end of the spindle. Wrap the cord around the spindle and put the drill in position. Pull the two ends of the cord down and outward, which causes the spindle to rotate. This tool can be used for drilling holes or starting fires by friction like the fire stick. My guess is that the cord drill was invented by people playing with a drop spindle. Twisting the string around the spindle and then pulling both ends causes rapid spinning, followed by a winding up again. After this was observed, people would have used the device for drilling holes and starting fires.

TOOLS AND MATERIALS

1 soft flat round stone that can be easily shaped or clay (for the flywheel)

1 pointed stone

1 Drop Spindle (see page 78)

Stone Blade (page 16)

Cordage (page 76; made from plant fiber, for the cord)

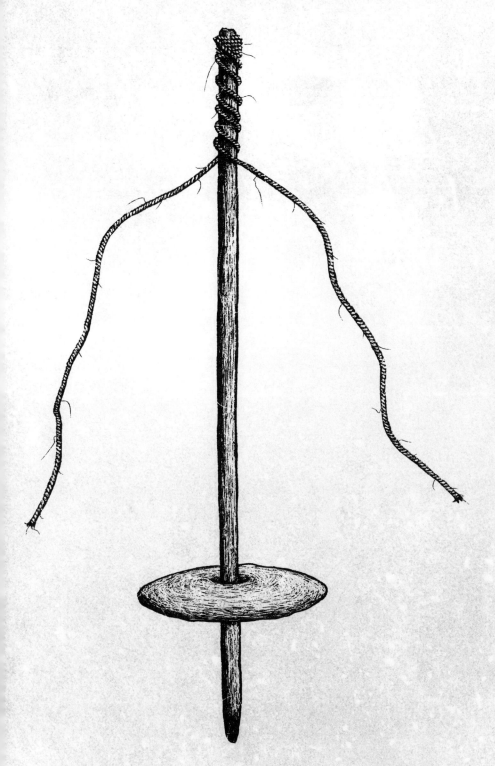

1. The flywheel should be big enough to hold the momentum of the spinning stick but not so big as to be unwieldy; 4 to 6 inches (10 to 15 cm) will do for a small drill. Use a sharp stone to shape the stone or mold clay by hand to the chosen size.

2. To make the flywheel, use the pointed stone to peck a hole through the soft flat round stone (A). If using clay, dry out the shaped clay and fire it.

3. Slip the flywheel over the narrow end of the spindle and wedge it tightly in place (B).

4. Use the stone blade to carve a notch in the top of the spindle to fit the cord.

5. Make some cordage and then fit the middle of the cord into the notch at the top of the spindle (C).

HOW TO UPGRADE A CORD DRILL INTO A PUMP DRILL

This upgraded version of the cord drill has a crossbar that is pumped up and down to create a drilling motion. Like the cord drill, the pump drill can be used both for drilling holes in stone or wood if a stone bit is attached to the end of the spindle and for making fire by friction.

1. Choose a piece of wood to be the crossbar about 20 inches (50 cm) long; use a sharp stone to mark its center.

2. Use the sharp stone to gouge a hole in the center of the crossbar. The hole should be large enough for the spindle to fit through so that it can spin freely at its thickest end.

3. Take the cord off the spindle; slip the crossbar over it.

4. Raise the bar to just above the flywheel. Put the cord back on the spindle.

5. Use a hand axe or stone blade to cut a piece of wood to half the length of the cord when it is tied in place to form a 60-60-60-degree-angle triangle (see step 7).

6. Use a stone blade to carve notches into the ends of the crossbar where the cord ends will be tied.

7. Tie the cord ends to the notches in the crossbar. The cord and crossbar should form a 60-60-60-degree-angle triangle.

8. Turn the spindle so that the cord wraps around the spindle, which causes the crossbar to slide up the spindle. When the cord is completely wound up, put the end of the spindle into the object to be drilled and push the crossbar downward. This causes the cord to unravel and makes the spindle spin rapidly.

9. When the cord is completely unwound, the momentum of the flywheel wraps the cord back around the spindle, drawing the crossbar back up the shaft. Allow the bar to rise to its beginning position, then push the bar back down to repeat the process in the opposite direction.

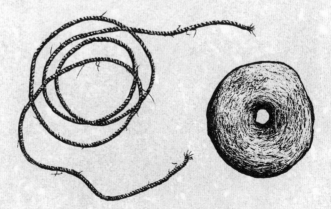

WATER HAMMER

HOW TO USE
A WATER HAMMER

Put the objects to be crushed on the mortar. The hammer will lift and drop many times per day as the water flows to crush the materials.

A water hammer is a machine that converts the energy of falling water into a hammering motion. It consists of a waterspout, a hammer that sits on a pivot, and a mortar where the hammer strikes. The end of the hammer placed near the spout has a trough to collect the water from the spout. As the trough fills up to the point of overflowing, the hammer end overbalances and the hammerhead lifts up. The water then tips out of the trough, and the hammerhead falls onto the mortar. This invention probably originated in ancient China and is predated by a similar foot-operated hammer that was adapted to be powered by falling water rather than the user's foot.

TOOLS AND MATERIALS

Celt Axe (page 94)

1 large log about 6.5 feet (2 m) long (for the main body of the hammer)

Mallet & Chisel (page 22)

1 small log about 2 feet (50 cm) long and 4 inches (10 cm) wide (for the hammerhead)

Adze (page 90)

Blowpipe (page 34)

Smaller pieces of wood (for the tripod and crossbar; any wood will do, as long as it is strong enough to support the weight of the hammer)

Cane, vines, or Cordage (page 76; for the lashings)

Any tough stone or wood (for mortar)

Half a hollow log to act as a water spout

1. To make the main body of the hammer, use the Celt axe to cut down the large log. Use the chisel to carve a mortise in the end of the large log for the hammerhead.

2. To make the hammerhead, use the Celt axe to cut down the small log; insert it into the mortise carved in the end of the large log.

3. Use the mallet and chisel to carve a mortise in the middle of the large log to act as the pivot. Use the blowpipe and hot coals to help burn the mortice (to save cutting).

4. Use the adze to carve a trough in the other end of the large log to catch the water (A). Use hot coals and blowpipe to help shape the trough by charring and scraping the wood away.

5. Use the smaller pieces of wood to make a tripod; use cane, vines, or cordage to lash the pieces together. Slip the crossbar through the mortise in the middle of the hammer, and lash the crossbar to the tripod. The hammer will now balance like a seesaw (B).

6. Find half a hollow log (one split down the middle). Put the waterspout into the stream to create a waterfall.

7. Position the trough of the hammer under the spout. As water fills the trough and empties out, the hammer will lift and fall by itself (C).

8. Make a mortar from stone or wood by shaping a depression in the stone with a hammer stone or cutting/ burning a hole in wood with an adze and blowpipe and placing it under the hammer (D).

SHELTER

112	DRYSTONE WALL
116	MUD WALL
120	WATTLE & DAUB WALL
126	DOME HUT
132	GABLED ROOF HUT
140	A-FRAME HUT
146	ROUND HUT
152	PYRAMIDAL HUT
156	CHIMNEY
160	ONDOL

DRYSTONE WALL

A drystone wall consists of two faces of stone with a heart of smaller stones and rubble at the center: mortar is not used to hold it together. The weight and friction of the stones keep it standing. The first huts I ever built had drystone walls because they were easy to construct.

TOOLS AND MATERIALS

Digging Stick (page 20)

A pile of flat stones of
  various sizes (see Tips)

Hammer Stone (page 14)

WHEN TO BUILD A DRYSTONE WALL

Build a drystone wall when suitable mortar isn't available or when good building stone is abundant. A well-built drystone wall can stand for hundreds of years without maintenance. It is also possible to make a circular hut from a drystone wall with an inward curve to form a dome so no roof is needed.

TIPS

Round river stones will roll off each other and will not be fit for use without shaping.

The foundation stones should be strong enough to bear the weight of the stones laid above them.

1. Use the digging stick to dig a shallow trench and mark off the base of the wall.

2. Put the largest flat stones in the trench first so that they provide a strong foundation (A).

3. The flat face of each stone should face out to form the flat face of the wall. The rest of the stone will be hidden inside the wall, so its shape doesn't matter (B).

4. For each layer, build both the inner and outer faces of the wall. Each stone should sit on the joint between two stones laid below it. Fill in any gaps between the two faces with smaller stones. Continue adding layers until the wall is as high as you want it to be (C).

5. If any of the stones don't quite fit, shape them with the hammer stone so that they fit into the gap.

MUD WALL

This type of wall is basically built straight up from the ground. Mud is piled in layers to form a solid construction that becomes hard when dried. Mud walls need protection from the rain; otherwise, they will dissolve back into mud. For this reason, in wet areas, it's sometimes better to construct a roof first on posts before building the mud wall that will envelop it. I often use mud walls for huts because the materials for building them are on-site. Digging up the soil will also leave a drain or a pit that can be useful for controlling the flow and storage of water.

TOOLS AND MATERIALS

Digging Stick (page 20)

Water

1 pot (for carrying water to the soil site)

Fibrous material (for mixing with the mud if it starts to crack)

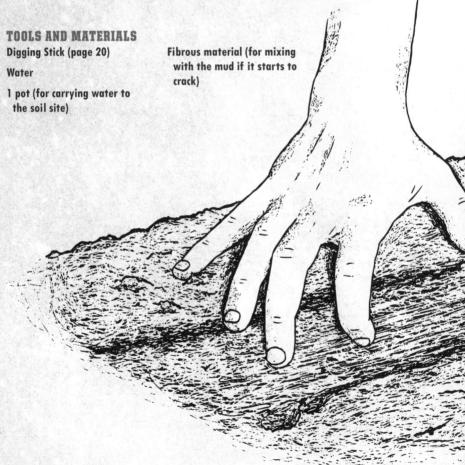

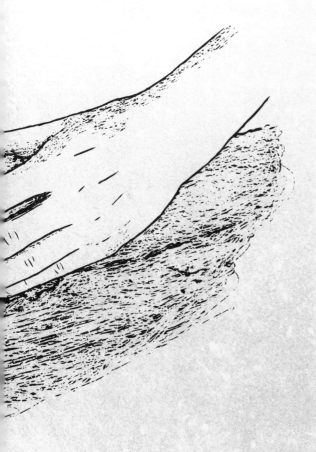

TIPS

When starting a mud wall, it can be helpful to put down a layer of stones to prevent rising damp from entering the wall.

A mud wall needs to be protected from rain, so make sure that the eaves of the roof covering the structure protrude enough to shed water.

It is a good idea to dig the soil so that it forms a trench around the building, if possible, to aid drainage.

1. Use the digging stick to excavate the soil; mix with water to form mud (A). If the mud you're using cracks as it dries, add fibrous material to it before building the wall. Sprinkle the material over the mud and then stomp the fiber into it (B).

2. Pile the mud in a layer as wide as you intend the wall to be. Add stones to the mud if possible to lessen the amount of mud required for the wall (C). Wait until the previous layer is stiff before adding new layers; otherwise, the wall will slump.

3. To speed up the drying process, start a fire (see page 33) in the center of the room so that the heat radiates out to all walls.

WATTLE & DAUB WALL

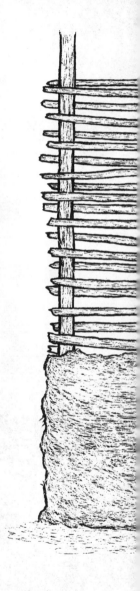

Wattle and daub is a composite of woven saplings or cane that is used to construct a wall and then covered with mud on both sides. The mud is flung into the wattles so that it sticks securely to the structure; it is then allowed to dry in place and harden. This type of wall needs protection from termites and rain to prevent the mud from dissolving. It is quicker to build than a solid mud wall and requires less material, but it's thinner and not as strong.

TOOLS AND MATERIALS

Adze (page 90) or Celt Axe (page 94)

Timber (for the upright posts) as tall as the wall is to be, plus at least 10 inches (25 cm) to go underground

Hammer Stone (page 14)

Saplings or branches that are durable but thin enough to weave with

Digging Stick (page 20)

Water

1 pot (for carrying water)

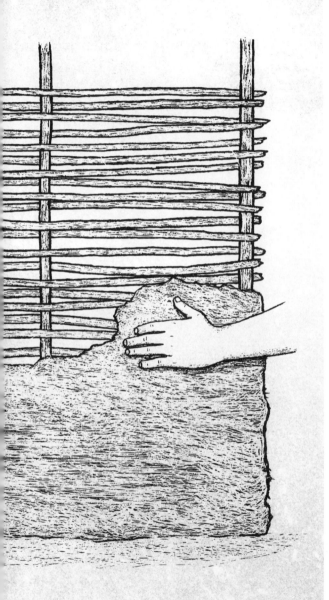

TIPS

Start a fire (see page 33) in the hut to assist with the drying process.

TIPS

Start a fire (see page 33) in the hut to assist with the drying process.

This wall will last as long as water is kept off it. Roof eaves should extend outward so that rain is thrown away from the mud on the walls.

Wattle and daub walls can be broken to allow openings for windows or fireplaces.

1. Use an adze or a Celt axe to cut the timber for the upright posts. Use the hammer stone to hammer the posts into the ground about 10 inches (25 cm) apart to form the intended wall of the structure (A).

2. Weave flexible saplings in and out between these posts so that they form a basketlike structure (B).

3. Use the digging stick to dig up the soil around the hut and mix with water to form mud. Apply the mud to the wattle walls by throwing it on and smoothing it in place (C).

4. If mud falls off the wall, add it in layers: allow each layer to dry slightly before applying the next.

TERMITES!

Be wary of termites when building structures from wood. In colder climates, this will be less of a problem, but in the warmer, wet tropical regions you can bet these pesky creatures will quickly start breaking down your structures. Find a site without them, if possible, by searching for signs of them: the covered tunnels they build into trees or their nests on the ground. You can deter termites somewhat by taking cooled wood ash from the fireplace of the shelter and spreading it around the bases of the posts of the shelters. Provided the ash stays dry, it will repel the termites as soon as they encounter it because of its caustic nature. Other than this trick, I know of few natural termite repellents. If you find yourself in a termite-occupied area and there is no way around it, avoid building wooden structures in the first place. Go for stone instead.

HOW TO MAKE ASH CEMENT

Ash cement is made from the ashes of wood bark and leaves combined with aggregate such as sand or crushed pottery; it sets hard after 3 days and will not dissolve in water after this time. The calcium oxide in the ash becomes hydrated when mixed with water; when exposed to air during the setting period it becomes calcium carbonate. Aluminum oxide and silica present in the ash contribute pozzolans that strengthen the cement over time. I developed ash cement because the only access to limestone I had to make cement was in shells, but this amount was too small to use for that purpose.

Bark and leaves

Updraft Kiln (page 176)

Water

**Pots (for carrying water
to mix the cement)**

**Aggregate such as sand,
gravel, or crushed
terra-cotta**

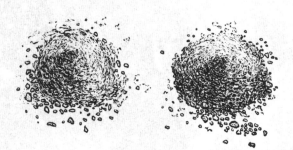

1. Burn large amounts of bark and leaves on the grate of the kiln (A). The temperature must be very high for the bark and leaves to convert completely to ash with hardly any charcoal.

2. Add only enough water to the ash to make it into a workable paste (start with a water-to-ash ratio of 1:2).

3. Mix the paste with the aggregate (B) and form it into shape (for example, a brick). It can also be used as a mortar for joining bricks together.

4. The cement should be set after 3 days, but it's best to let it dry completely if it isn't.

5. Test the dry cement in water (C); it should not dissolve.

DOME HUT

OPTIMAL SETUP FOR A DOME HUT

A small fire in the middle of the hut should keep the whole area warm. A raised bed can be built at the back of the shelter and dry firewood can be stored just inside the doorway. Tools can be stored under the bed out of the way. The dome forms a pointed arch profile that is halfway between a true dome and a tepee, giving it a good internal volume, while the pointed top sheds rain effectively while funneling smoke up and through the thatch at the top, away from the occupant.

A dome hut is a shelter made of cut saplings with their bottom ends inserted into the ground to form a circle and their upper ends lashed together to form a pointed dome. This frame is then thatched to make a comfortable small shelter to sleep in and store tools out of the weather. The earliest domes were likely made from pliable saplings, followed by mud domes and eventually masonry domes.

TOOLS AND MATERIALS

1 radius stick, 4 feet (1.25 cm) long (optional)

Hammer Stone (page 14)

9 marker stakes, about 10 inches (25 cm) long

Hand Axe (page 18)

8 flexible saplings, 9 feet (2.75 m) long

Digging Stick (page 20)

Stone Blade (page 16)

Vines or Cordage (page 76; for lashing; a lot is required, so cut as needed)

Thatching material, such as palm fronds (400 fronds), long grass (cut as needed; you will also need saplings to attach the grass), or sheets of bark (cut as needed)

1. Clear a circular space 8 feet (2.5 m) in diameter (A). Use the radius stick to mark off the circle if you want.

2. Use the hammer stone to hammer 1 stake into the ground to mark the center of the circle; then hammer the other 8 stakes spaced equally apart around the edge of the circle to mark where the saplings will go (B).

3. Use the hand axe to cut the 8 flexible saplings for the frame.

4. Use the hammer stone and digging stick to make 8 postholes 10 inches (25 cm) deep for the saplings. Make sure the holes are just wide enough for the saplings to fit neatly into them.

5. Stick the 8 saplings into the holes (C).

6. Use the stone blade to cut some vines; lash the tops of the saplings together with the vines. Tie them together in opposing pairs so that there is even tension while you assemble the frame; this will maintain an even shape for the dome (D).

7. Use the stone blade to cut palm fronds for thatch and then split them with your hands (E). Lash the split pairs, with the leaflets facing down, to the frame of the dome. If long grass is chosen as the thatching material, use the hand axe to cut 8 saplings and lash them to the frame horizontally before lashing the grass to them.

8. Leave an opening about 2.5 feet (75 cm) tall and 2.5 feet (75 cm) wide in the front of the dome so that you can crawl inside.

9. When the hut is nearly complete, make a conical cap by making a tepee of sticks on the ground (F), thatch it, and lift it onto the top of the dome with a long pole to keep out the rain.

10. Use the digging stick to dig a fire pit in the center of the hut; it is now ready to use.

HOW TO MAKE A BARK ROOF

With few exceptions, removing all of the bark from live trees will often kill them. From a sustainability and forest conservation point of view, paperbark is the most suitable to be used for bark roofing, because removing the outer layer of dead bark won't kill the tree. Depending on the tree species, bark roofing will last for years.

1. Use a hand axe to cut a line down the tree trunk and cut around the circumference of the tree at the top and bottom of this cut.

2. Use a sharp stick to carefully lift the bark away from the trunk so that the bark comes off in large panels. Bark from small trees can be cut into small shingles.

3. To attach the panels to the roof, use a stone blade to make holes in the top of the panels and tie them to the wooden roof frame with vine or cordage so the next panel higher up covers the holes in the lower panel, to prevent water from getting in. Or weigh down bark panels with wooden jockeys (panes of timber lashed together at one end) that prevent the wind from blowing them away.

Bark roofing is quite watertight and will shed rain at lower roof pitches. Take care not to kill trees that would otherwise be left standing. For example, use the bark from the trees you cut down to make the hut for roofing. When removing bark from species that constantly regenerate bark (e.g., paperbark), do not cut down to the living layer as this will kill the tree. Trees use bark to keep out insect pests, so take only as much as you need—don't overharvest.

GABLED ROOF HUT

This small permanent hut is a simple square dwelling with a gabled roof and only enough area for a comfortable bed and storage space for tools and firewood. The ridgeline, or highest point, of the hut will be as high as the builder can reach comfortably; this project is based on a reach of 6.5 feet (2 m). The floor plan of the hut will be as long and wide as the ridge is tall (in this case, 6.5 feet [2 m] long and 6.5 feet [2 m] wide). The side walls will be half the height of the ridgeline so that the roof forms an angle of 45 degrees to shed rain well with most roofing materials. Build several small gabled roof huts for different purposes – living, storage, workshop – instead of building one large hut.

TOOLS AND MATERIALS

Celt Axe (page 94)

2 poles, each at least 7 feet (2.25 m) long (for the ridge posts; see Tip)

Digging Stick (page 20)

Hammer Stone (page 14)

4 poles, each at least 4 feet (1.25 m) long (for the wall posts)

3 poles, each 8 feet (2.5 m) long (for the roof beams)

Cordage (page 76) or vines (for lashing)

10 rafters, each 5.75 feet (1.75 cm) long (to go on the roof beams)

Roofing material: thatch, such as grass-covered battens or palm fronds, or bark, ceramic, or barrel tiles (see pages 130, 138, 139, and 145)

Material for the walls: wattle and daub (see page 120; wooden stakes, cane or green twigs, soil, and water are also needed), thatch (see page 145), or mud (see page 116; water and pots for carrying water are also needed; extend the length of the eaves by 10 inches [25 cm] to cover them. In taller structures make the eves wider still.)

TIP

Any type of wood will do as long as it's strong enough to support the hut's roof.

OPTIMAL SETUP FOR A GABLED ROOF HUT

For use as a shelter, put a bed 2.5 feet (75 cm) wide and 5.75 feet (1.75 m) long on the side of the hut without the door and fireplace. The space under the bed can be used to store tools and some materials. Store firewood next to the fireplace. Use the rest of the area as a small workspace. A hut like this made without walls can serve as a woodshed to store firewood and charcoal.

1. Use the Celt axe to cut wood for the ridge posts (A). Ten inches (25 cm) of the posts will be underground, so if the soil is soft, make the posts longer so that the structure will be more stable.

2. Use the digging stick to make 2 postholes at each end of the hut. Add the posts and use the hammer stone to knock them in (B).

3. Use the Celt axe to cut the wood for the wall posts. Use the digging stick to make 4 postholes at each corner of the hut. Put in the posts and use the hammer stone to knock them in. The posts should stand 3 feet (1 m) above the ground.

4. Use the Celt axe to cut the wood for the roof beams. Use cordage or vines to lash them to the ridge posts and wall posts. They should extend about 10 inches (25 cm) beyond the hut's front and back to form eaves to protect the walls (C).

5. Use the Celt axe to cut wood for the rafters and use cordage or vines to lash them to the roof beams. They should extend about 10 inches (25 cm) past the sides of the hut to form eaves (D).

6. Use cordage or vines to lash grass-covered battens, palm fronds, or another thatching material to the roof; start at the eaves so they'll shed rain and move up to the ridgeline to cover the roof. See pages 130, 138, 139, and 145 for instructions on finishing the roof.

7. Once the roof is finished and provides shelter from the rain, build the walls. For durable wattle and daub walls, use the hammer stone to hammer in 9 stakes 4 feet (1.25 m) long about 10 inches (25 cm) apart so they form the uprights of the wall. Weave the cane or green twigs between them, leaving a 3-foot (1 m) gap for a door on one side of the central ridge post at the front of the hut (E). Also leave a 20-inch (50 cm) square hole for a fireplace, if required, opposite the doorway.

8. With the frame complete, use the digging stick to dig a trench around the hut to get the soil for the mud. Using pots, carry water from a creek or wait until rain fills the trench and mix the mud on-site. Apply the mud to the wattle walls by throwing it on and smoothing it into place (F).

HOW TO PLACE TILES ON A GABLED ROOF HUT

Use a hand axe to cut wood to make the purlins for the roof; they should be about 4.5 inches (11.5 cm) long, a bit less than half the length of the tiles. Work on one side of the roof at a time. Install one layer of tiles by hooking the tabs over the purlins. Then lay the next layer so that the tiles cover any gaps between the previous layer to prevent water from getting in. Friction and gravity will work to keep the tiles sitting on the purlins; they will be quite secure in the absence of very strong winds. When you reach the top of the roof, lay the last layer over the ridgeline. Continue on the other side of the roof; hook the last layer over the top of the tiles on the other side. Cover the ridgeline with cap tiles to finish off the roof, making sure that they overlap any vertical gaps in the flat tiles they cover.

HOW TO MAKE FLAT CERAMIC ROOF TILES

I started making tiles for the roofs of my huts when I noticed that the thatch roofs rotted in wet weather. Made of nonperishable fired clay, flat rectangular ceramic roof tiles are resistant to fire and water and will not rot. This type of roof tile often has a tab on its underside that fits onto a wooden frame to form a structure's roof.

1. Split a length of loya cane or a sapling in half; this can be done by hand. Kink the cane without breaking it so that it forms the corners of a mold for the flat roof tile. Then lash the two ends together with vines or cordage to form a rectangular mold 10 inches (25 cm) long and 6 inches (15 cm) wide.

2. Find a flat rock for the mold to sit on while the tiles are formed. When the clay is homogenously mixed and at an optimal consistency for molding, dust the flat stone with wood ash, place the tile mold onto it, press the clay into the mold, and smooth it out. Form tabs at the top end of the tile so that it will sit on the roof purlins. Balance the mold with the clay inside vertically against a wooden stake to dry. When dry to the touch, take the tile out of the mold and set it aside to finish drying out completely. Dry it next to a fire if the humidity is high. Repeat the process until you have used up all the clay. To form the cap tiles that go along the ridge of a roof, take a flat tile without a tab and bend it over a log while it is still wet. Let it dry to the touch, then take it off the log and set it aside to finish drying out completely.

3. Once the tiles are bone-dry, place them in a kiln; collect 1 to 3 times the tiles' weight in wood to fire it. Collect more wood than you need so that you don't run out halfway through. Fire the tiles until all parts of them glow at least red-hot; tiles at the top of the kiln will be the last to heat up. When you are satisfied that they are properly fired, block the firebox entry and let them cool down in the kiln.

HOW TO MAKE BARREL ROOF TILES

I switched from flat tiles to barrel tiles for the roofs of my huts because I wanted to reduce the amount of wood I used. Because barrel tiles are longer than flat tiles and they are not staggered when laid, they can span a longer distance between purlins. Barrel roof tiles resemble half pipes. They taper from one end to the other so that they fit into the layer below them. Each layer of tiles fits over the subsequent one to cover any gaps between the tiles below. Barrel tiles are made with a mold and a frame to give them their curved shape.

1. Split in half a length of loya cane by hand or a sapling with a hand axe. Kink the cane without breaking it so that it forms the corners of a trapezoidal mold for the barrel roof tile. Then lash the two ends together with vines or cordage to form a trapezoidal mold 20 inches (50 cm) long and 8 inches (20 cm) wide at the long end and 6 inches (15 cm) wide at the short end.

2. Use a hand axe to cut wood from a log to make a pipe-shaped form for curving the tile. It should taper slightly to one end. If you can find a piece of wood in this shape already that will help.

3. Find a flat rock for the mold to sit on while the tiles are formed. Place the wooden form next to it. When the clay is homogenously mixed and at an optimal consistency for molding, dust the flat stone with wood ash, place the tile mold onto it, press the clay into the mold, and smooth it out.

4. Slide the tile in its mold off the rock and onto the form sitting next to it, removing the mold in the process.

5. Smooth the tile onto the form, giving it a curved shape. Then slide the tile off the form and onto the ground to dry. Repeat the process until you have used up all the clay.

6. Once the tiles are bone-dry, place them upright in a kiln; collect 1 to 3 times the tiles' weight in wood to fire it. Collect more wood than you need so that you don't run out halfway through. Fire the tiles until all parts of them glow at least red-hot; tiles at the top of the kiln will be the last to heat up. When you are satisfied that they are properly fired, block the firebox entry and let them cool down in the kiln.

HOW TO USE BARREL ROOF TILES ON A GABLED ROOF HUT

Place the tiles onto the purlins of the roof in vertical rows. The narrow end of each tile should face down onto the broad end of the tile below so that water moves from one tile to the next. Lay two rows in this manner, with the curves of the tiles facing up next to each other. Then place another row, with its broad end facing down, covering the gap between these two rows.

A-FRAME HUT

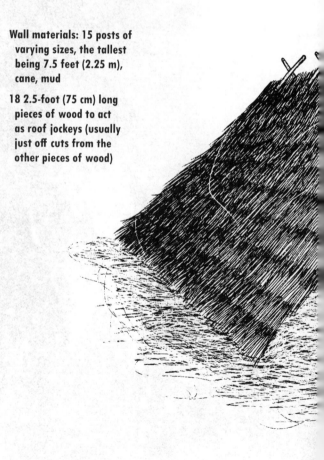

An A-frame hut is like a large roof built directly on the ground: a simple structure consisting of a ridgeline going from front to back with rafters extending down to the ground. Its dimensions – about 6.5 feet (2 m) tall in the center, 13 feet (4 m) wide, and 13 feet (4 m) long – give a pitch of 45 degrees to shed rain well. A person can walk right down the center of the hut without ducking; the sides that are too small to stand in can be used for storing firewood, tools, and other materials.

TOOLS AND MATERIALS

Hard Axe (page 18) or
  Celt Axe (page 94)

1 rear post, about 7 feet
  (2.25 m) long

1 ridgepole, about 13 feet
  (4 m) long

18 poles, each about 10 feet
  (3 m) long (for the rafters)

Hammer Stone (page 14)

Cordage (page 76) or cane (for
  lashing)

Thatch, such as palm fronds
  (1,200 if using), long grass,
  or bark shingles (cut as
  needed)

Wall materials: 15 posts of
  varying sizes, the tallest
  being 7.5 feet (2.25 m),
  cane, mud

18 2.5-foot (75 cm) long
  pieces of wood to act
  as roof jockeys (usually
  just off cuts from the
  other pieces of wood)

OPTIMAL SETUP FOR AN A-FRAME HUT

Use as a shelter or a workspace. Put a bed at the back or along one side. Store firewood, tools, and materials along the sides where it's too low to stand. Keep the center clear except for a stove or a fire pit so that you can easily walk down the length of the hut. The front of the structure is left open in warm climates to let in light.

TIP

Use thatch roofing to keep any hut or workspace dry and to protect it from the elements. Thatch is flammable, so be careful with fire. A small fire kept at least 6.5 feet (2 m) below the grass thatch should be safe, although in very dry weather it's probably best to keep the fire outside or contained within a chimney. After about 3 years in wet weather the thatch will probably need to be replaced.

1. Use the axe to cut the wood for the rear post, ridgepole, and rafters. Use the hammer stone to hammer in the rear post 10 inches (25 cm) deep. Use the cordage or cane to lash one end of the ridgepole to the rear post.

2. Use the cordage or cane to lash 2 rafters together to form an A-frame. Tie the other end of the ridgepole to the frame. Lay the other rafters onto the ridgepole and lash them down (A).

3. Split the palm fronds; use cordage or vine to lash them to the frame (B).

4. Lay fronds on the ridge and weigh them down by setting panes of timber lashed together at one end over the fronds. These are called jockeys because they resemble riders on horseback.

5. Make a wall to close up the back gable end (C). Use the axe to cut wood for the posts. Use the hammer stone to hammer in the posts about 10 inches (25 cm) deep and weave cane in and out to form a wattle frame. Plaster over the wattle with mud.

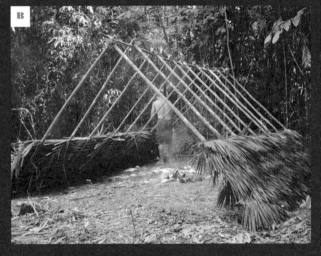

HOW TO MAKE A GRASS THATCH ROOF

Used by many cultures for thousands of years, grass thatching consists of bundles of grass laid over battens. To lay grass thatching, start at the base of the roof and overlap the bundles in such a way that they shed rain. It is a common roofing material in areas such as plains or open woodlands that have long grass. Grass thatching makes quick water-proof roofs, but it is perishable and may need replacing every 3 years or so if the climate is wet. Take care to keep sparks from fire away from the dry grass.

Stone Blade (page 16)

Long grasses or reeds (for thatching; long-stem species are a good choice because they will require fewer thatched battens than shorter species; I use Guinea grass, but substitute a similar grass that grows in your area)

Timber (for the battens; it should be not much thicker than a finger; the number necessary will depend on the size of the hut)

Strong vines or long grass twisted into Cordage (page 76) or yarn (for lashing)

1. Use the stone blade to cut the long grass at ground level, leaving the roots in the ground so that the grass will resprout.

2. Let the grass dry (if put on the hut when green, the grass will dry and shrink). Use the stone blade to cut the battens so that they will fit the roof rafters, which should be about 3 feet (1 m) apart.

3. Use the grass cordage or vines to tie the grass onto the battens. Attach the battens to the rafters of the hut using grass cordage or vines; start at the base of the roof and overlap new layers as you move up. Space them at least half the length of the grass being used for the roof.

4. Cover the ridgeline with thatched battens so that they overlap each side.

ROUND HUT

This hut has a circular floor plan, a cylinder forming the walls, and a conical roof. The roof angle is 45 degrees to shed rain effectively. A central fire pit is used to heat and light the structure. A smoke hole or chimney is not necessary; the smoke diffuses through the thatch. (In fact, a smoke hole would increase the draft, which could cause a fire.) The origin of round huts probably stems from the need to conserve materials when building: a circle contains more area per perimeter than a square. A round hut loses less heat for the same reason.

TOOLS AND MATERIALS

Celt Axe (page 94)

12 posts, about 6.5 feet (2 m) long (for the wall)

12 poles, about 3 feet (1 m) long (for the lintels)

12 poles, about 8 feet (2.5 m) long (for the roof)

Hammer Stone (page 14)

Cordage (page 76), cane, or vines (for lashing; a lot is required, so cut as needed)

Thatching material, such as palm fronds (800 fronds), long grass, or sheets of bark

Cane or saplings (for wattle wall)

Digging Stick (page 20)

Mud (for walls)

3 6.5-foot-long (2 m) pieces of wood for tripod ladder

1 3-foot-long (1 m) piece of wood for ladder step

1 10-foot-long (3 m) pole to lift roof cap into place

OPTIMAL SETUP FOR A ROUND HUT

The hut is used for living and working. Store firewood in the hut; place a bed in the back behind the fire. The smoke diffusing through the thatch helps preserve it and keeps insect pests out. There's room to put a low kiln in the center of the hut if there is no risk of fire.

1. Use the Celt axe to cut wood for the wall posts, lintels, and roof poles.

2. Use the hammer stone to hammer the 12 wall posts about 20 inches (50 cm) into the ground so they are about 5 feet (1.5 m) above the ground. Use the cordage, cane, or vines to lash the lintels to the posts (A).

3. Build a tripod ladder and place it in the center of the hut. Tie three pieces of wood together at one end and spread them out into a tripod. Then tie the 3-foot (1 m) piece of wood to this to act as the ladder step (B).

4. Use the cordage, cane, or vines to lash the 12 roof poles to the walls, with about 14.75 inches (37.5 cm) overhanging the wall for eaves.

5. Use cordage, cane, or vines to tie the ends of the roof poles together at the top to form the conical roof (C).

6. Thatch the roof (D; see page 150); use the ladder to climb up. Make a roof cap from thatch and lift it into place with a long pole so it sits on top (E).

7. Weave cane or saplings between the wall posts to form a wattle and daub wall (see page 120). Leave a gap for a doorway if required.

8. Use the digging stick to dig a moat around the drip line of the roof eaves.

9. Use the excavated soil to make mud and daub the walls with it.

10. Dig a fire pit in the center of the hut floor. Light a fire to help dry the walls.

HOW TO MAKE A PALM THATCH ROOF

Palm thatching uses split palm fronds to shed rain. In jungles and tropical rain forests, the palms have drip tips on their leaves, an adaptation to the wet environment that sheds water to prevent algae from growing on the leaves and blocking sunlight.

Palm fronds (for thatching; any palm can be used as long as it has plentiful leaves along its spine; some species of palm will last longer than others, probably due to higher silica content in the leaves)

Stone Blade (page 16)

Vines, Cordage (page 76), or bark strips (for lashing)

1. Use the stone blade to cut a bunch of fronds and take them back to the hut site. The roof frame of the hut will have vertical rafters positioned a bit closer than the length of a palm frond.

2. With your hands, carefully split the fronds evenly down the middle from the end to the base (A).

3. Cross the 2 halves of the palm frond over so that the leaves hang down; use vines, cordage, or bark strips to lash them to the rafters (B).

4. Continue to lay the thatch along the rafters until 1 layer is complete. Then begin the next layer, slightly overlapping the first layer, moving up the rafters. The overlapping leaves will shed rain (C).

A

B

C

TIP

Use palm thatching in an area with full sun to prevent mold growth. To stop grubs and insects from moving in and eating the thatch, make a smoky fire in the fire pit from time to time. The insects will leave the thatch and a coating of creosote from the smoke will make it unpalatable to them, increasing the life span of the roof.

PYRAMIDAL HUT

A pyramidal hut stands on four posts to form a square roof that comes to a point at the top. This type of hut is wind resistant and needs fewer posts than a gabled roof hut. The shape of the roof funnels smoke from a central fire pit to the apex. Trapping the smoke benefits a thatch roof: it coats the leaves and acts as an insect repellent, which in turn increases the life span of the material.

TOOLS AND MATERIALS

Digging Stick (page 20)

Celt Axe (page 94)

4 corner posts, about 8 feet (2.5 m) long (see Tip)

Hammer Stone (page 14)

4 roof beams, about 10 feet (3 m) long (see Tip)

Lawyer cane, Cordage (page 76), or vines (for lashing; cut it as necessary)

4 poles, about 11.5 feet (3.5 m) long (for pyramid ridges)

Palm fronds or grass (for roof thatching; cut it as necessary)

Rafters, 13 x 10.5 feet (4 x 3.25 m), 26 x 9 feet (8 x 2.75 m), 26 x 5.75 feet (8 x 1.75 m), and 26 x 2.5 feet (8 x 0.75m)

4 poles 13 feet (4 m) long (to form the roof edge)

Timber for the posts and beams must be thick enough to bear the weight of the worker and strong enough to support the roof. A lot of wood will be needed; cut it as necessary.

THE OPTIMAL SETUP FOR A PYRAMIDAL HUT

Windy locations are ideal sites for a pyramidal hut. The eaves encircle the whole structure, protecting the walls from driving rain. A central fire pit or furnace works well in this type of hut: the heat rises up to the apex and diffuses through the thatch, helping to preserve it from insects and mold. The best place for a bed is the ground floor of the hut; the second story can be too smoky for sleeping. Instead, store perishable materials on the second floor; rising smoke will act as a preservative.

1. Use the digging stick to mark off the floor plan of the hut. An area 10 feet (3 m) square is a good size.

2. Use the digging stick to dig postholes into the corners of the area at least 20 inches (50 cm) deep (A).

3. Use the Celt axe to cut wood for the corner posts. Use the hammer stone to hammer the corner posts into the ground so that they stand 6.5 feet (2 m) tall (B).

4. Use the Celt axe to cut wood for the roof beams. Use the lawyer cane to lash the roof beams horizontally to the top of the posts using square lashing (C). These beams will support the platform that will go on top of the posts.

5. Lay more beams onto the top of this so that it forms a second-story platform. These will form the floor of the attic of the hut. Use as many beams as needed to cover the platform.

6. Use the Celt axe to cut wood for the pyramid ridges. Attach the pyramid ridges to the platform using lashings. They will extend over the sides of the platform to create eaves. Then tie the 4 top ends of the pyramid ridges together to form the point of the pyramid (D).

7. Use the lawyer cane to lash the rafters to the roof frame so that they are 20 inches (50 cm) apart to support the thatching (E). Make an edge around the eaves of the roof using the four 13-foot (4 m) poles for the first layer of thatch to lie on. Thatch the whole roof (see pages 145 and 150). Build a wall of your choosing (see pages 112–122) or leave the hut open as a covered workspace (F).

CHIMNEY

A chimney is a tube that funnels exhaust gases and smoke from a fireplace to the external atmosphere. The stack effect ensures that the hot smoke is drawn up and out of the building because it is more buoyant than the incoming combustion air. A fireplace is fitted with a chimney to keep the dwelling smoke-free and to make the fire burn more efficiently. I began using chimneys in my huts when smoke from fire pits irritated my eyes and lungs.

TOOLS AND MATERIALS

Stones (for fireplace base and top of chimney), collect as needed

Digging Stick (page 20)

Water

Pots (for carrying water to the building site)

Mud (see Tips)

Despite being flammable, logs can be used to build a chimney, but they must be caulked with mud or dirt to ensure a strong natural draft with no air gaps to short-circuit it. Rocks mortared together with mud will make a fine chimney, and you won't have to worry about its flammability.

The mud should be a mix of materials that won't crack too much as it dries. Most soil is a mix of clay and stone, but if it is very clayey it may shrink and crack excessively.

Build the chimney above roof height for a strong draft.

1. Leave a space for the fireplace at one end of the hut (A). Placing it opposite the door will draw a draft through the hut; placing it next to the door will draw cold drafts from the door into the fire and out through the chimney, keeping the room warmer.

2. Gather stones for the fireplace base; the stones will prevent rising damp from wetting the mud. Build the base as a U-shaped enclosure with the opening facing into the hut (B).

1. Use the digging stick to excavate soil; mix the soil with water to form mud. Plaster the mud over the wood covering the gap. Continue to build more layers with stone, wood, and mud; the width of the chimney should narrow with height (C). If the weather is wet, start a fire in it (see page 33) while building it so that the mud will dry faster.

2. To stop water from getting in, put a flat stone on top of the chimney and form a hole in the side of the chimney (while still wet) for smoke to exit, or rest the flat stone on 3 smaller stones (D). The flat stone will stabilize the 3 smaller ones.

ONDOL

An ondol ("hot stone" in Korean) is an underfloor heating system for dwellings. The simplest version can be described as having a fireplace at one end of a long tunnel covered with stones and mud. At the other end of the tunnel a chimney is positioned to create a draft pulling smoke from the fire along the underside of the stones, heating them as it goes. The floor then conducts heat to the occupant sitting on the surface or radiates it up into the dwelling. The firebox can be situated outside the dwelling so no smoke enters the room. I first used an ondol in a mud hut I built to help keep warm in cold weather.

TOOLS AND MATERIALS
Digging Stick (page 20)

Flat stones (for covering the trench and conducting heat)

Water

Pots (for carrying water)

Mud

HOW TO USE
AN ONDOL

Light a fire in the fireplace and fuel it with firewood. Do not use charcoal or coal: burning charcoal or coal produces carbon monoxide that could suffocate you while you are sleeping. Deaths attributed to ondols in twentieth-century Korea coincided with the introduction of coal briquettes. A good clean wood fire is safe. If in doubt, make a fire a few hours before going to sleep and rake out the fireplace so there is no risk. If heated sufficiently, the ondol will keep the dwelling warm until dawn.

1. Use the digging stick to dig a long trench in the room to be heated.

2. Cover the trench with large flat stones, leaving both ends open (A). Try to make the trench slant upward in the direction the smoke is intended to travel.

3. Mix the excavated soil with water to form mud; cover the trench stones with mud (B).

4. Build a small chimney outside the back end of the trench, usually at the back end of the hut (see page 156), about 2.5 to 3 feet (75 cm to 1 m) above the fireplace entry (C).

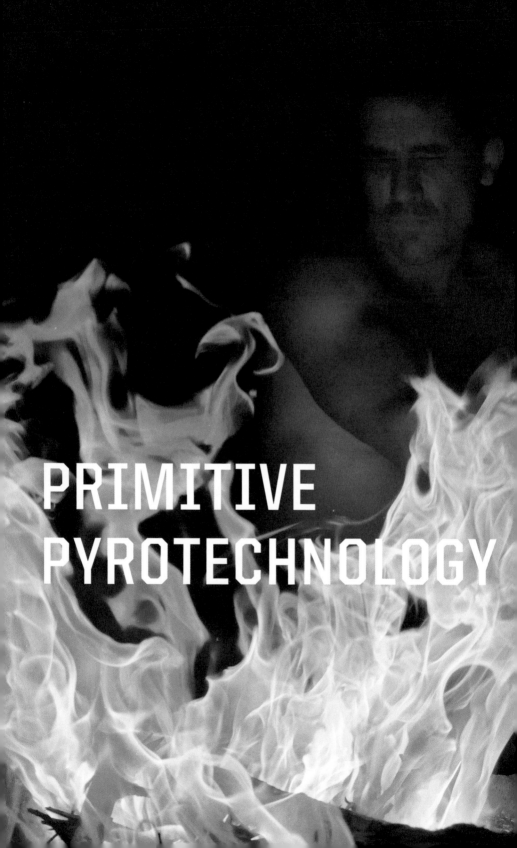

PRIMITIVE
PYROTECHNOLOGY

166   **REUSABLE CHARCOAL MOUND**

172   **IRON PRILLS**

176   **UPDRAFT KILN**

182   **NATURAL DRAFT FURNACE**

186   **FORGE BLOWER**

REUSABLE CHARCOAL MOUND

TIP

Pure clay, though good for pottery, may crack if used to build a charcoal mound. It's often better to use ordinary topsoil, which contains impurities such as loam and sand that help prevent the charcoal mound from cracking as it is heated and quickly dries.

Charcoal is a very useful material to have on hand out in the wild. Besides cooking, charcoal can be used for making pottery or even smelting iron (see page 172). A reusable charcoal mound will save you a lot of time: you won't have to build a new foundation each time you need to make another batch.

TOOLS AND MATERIALS

Digging Stick (page 20)

Ordinary loamy soil, sand, and clay

Water

1 pot (for carrying water)

Dry wood

Fire (see page 33)

Wooden Tongs (page 38)

Hand Axe (page 18)

Baskets (see pages 64, 68, and 72)

1. Use the digging stick to mix soil, sand, and clay with water to make mud (A).

2. Form the mud into a cylinder about 2.5 feet (75 cm) in diameter and at least 1.6 feet (50 cm) high (B).

3. Use the digging stick to make 8 holes evenly around the base of the furnace so that fresh air can get into the mound when it is lit. This will be the permanent part of the mound. Let the mud stiffen sufficiently before firing; otherwise, the shell of the mound will crack, letting in too much air.

4. Stack the dry wood tightly into the mound in a conical shape so that the large pieces are in the center and the thin pieces are on the outside. There will be some air gaps, but this is necessary to carry out the burn.

5. Continue to stack the wood so that it forms a cone about 45 degrees in slope above the wall of the mound (C).

6. Plaster mud over the cone so that there is only a small opening at the top of the cone for the hot

gases and smoke to exit. The mound is finished and is ready to light (D).

7. Light a fire and then put hot coals from it into the top of the mound, using tongs or sticks (E). Keep fanning the coals until the wood in the mound catches fire. The fire front will then burn back down the mound against the updraft. When fire reaches an airhole in the base of the mound, seal it up with mud to choke the fire so that it doesn't begin to burn the charcoal in the mound. When the last hole is sealed, close the hole in the top of the mound with mud. Let the mound cool completely; when it is cool to the touch, it should be ready to open.

8. Use the hand axe to break open the top of the mound; leave the cylinder intact. Take out the charcoal and store it in baskets in a dry shelter until you are ready to use it (F). Retain any unburned brands to refire for the next batch. Collect more wood and repeat the process whenever you need more charcoal.

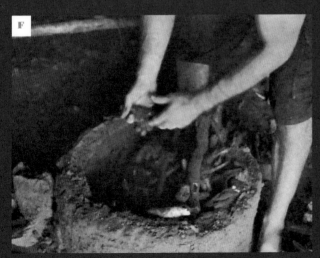

HOW TO MAKE CHARCOAL

1. Stack dry wood into a conical or domed mound with large pieces in the center and small ones to the outside. Stack the wood as tightly as possible. There will be some air gaps, but this is necessary to carry out the burn. Make small mounds first to practice if you wish. They can be several meters wide, but smaller ones won't take as long to fire. A mound that is 3 feet (1 m) in diameter is a good test size.

2. Dig the soil from around the mound; add water and mix to form mud. Plaster this mud on the mound, forming an airtight shell. Leave a vent hole in the top for the hot gases and smoke to exit. Make airholes evenly around the base of the mound so that fresh air can get into the mound when it is lit. Let the mud stiffen sufficiently before firing; otherwise, the shell of the mound will crack, letting in too much air.

3. When the mound is ready to fire, kindle the fire in the air exit at the top. It is known as an upside-down fire because it burns back down toward the ground. The descending fire front uses up the air entering the base, which allows only anoxic gases to reach the charcoal above, which remains unburned. These gases, though flammable, do not catch fire until they exit the top of the mound. Sometimes a flame will appear above the mound where these gases meet fresh air and combust.

4. The fire will continue to burn down toward the airholes. When the fire reaches the airholes it needs to be choked so that it doesn't begin to burn the charcoal in the mound. Have some mud ready to block the airholes. Keep looking in the airholes: when you see fire has reached them, simply block them with mud. Fire will reach the holes at different times; usually the holes on the windward side need to be blocked first. No guesswork is necessary: plug the holes when you see fire in them.

5. When the last airhole is blocked, seal up the air exit at the top of the mound with mud. Let the mound cool completely; when it is cool to the touch it should be ready to open. Break the mound open and take out the charcoal; store it in baskets in a dry shelter until you are ready to use it.

HOW TO MAKE POTTERY USING CHARCOAL

➤ In a pottery kiln, the fuel (usually wood) is kept separate in a firebox beneath the objects being heated. Charcoal can be used to fire pottery in an ordinary upright kiln, but it is most often used on its own in a packed fuel bed in direct contact with a single item of pottery.

➤ The charcoal is packed around a single pot (no greater than half the internal diameter of the kiln) on top of the perforated floor instead of being put in the firebox beneath the pot. This configuration allows the pot to reach such a high temperature that it will be fired to stoneware in a shorter time than it would take using wood fuel. A glaze should appear on the pot. Use only white clay; otherwise, the minerals in the clay will lower its melting point, causing the pot to slump or melt.

IRON PRILLS

Mixing the metal ore with the charcoal fuel bed and then forcing air into it will allow it to reach a high enough temperature to melt the ore. Charcoal also creates a reducing atmosphere, one rich in carbon monoxide to strip oxygen off the iron oxide converting it to metallic iron. If the fuel bed is tall enough and the lump size of the charcoal is small enough (though not so small as to prevent airflow through the bed).

The larger the charcoal lump the less air resistance and hence the higher the temperature. But less air resistance means more oxygen gets in, leading to oxidation (either turning the metal back into rust or preventing the oxide from turning to metal).

Iron bacteria reduce iron in the water table to stay alive; they precipitate as an orange slime. I used iron bacteria in my first attempts to smelt iron. One of my future experiments will be to cast the iron from these bacteria into a clay mold to determine whether it is sturdy enough to form implements.

TOOLS AND MATERIALS

Hammer Stone (page 14)

Charcoal (see page 166). One basket of charcoal (13 pounds [6 kg] minimum) is usually needed, always have extra in case a smelt runs longer or simply have a large pile next to the furnace.

Iron bacteria (found in waterlogged soils near creeks and waterways on every continent). Collect a minimum of 2 pounds (1 kg).

Digging Stick (page 20)

Forge Blower (page 186)

Natural Draft Furnace (page 182)

Mud

Dry wood

Clay to make a small pot to melt the iron prills into a larger ingot

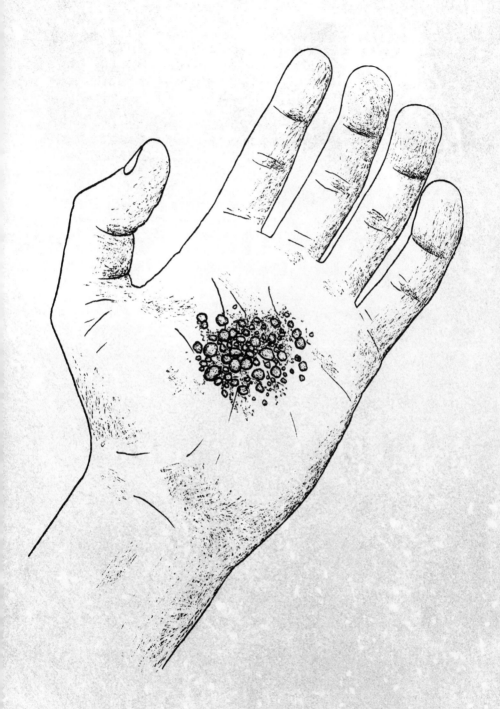

1. Use a hammer stone to crush the charcoal into a powder. Mix the iron bacteria with the crushed charcoal powder in a 1:1 proportion by volume. Roll the mixture into pellets about 1 inch (2.5 cm) in diameter (A).

2. Use a digging stick to dig a pit 10 inches (25 cm) wide and 10 inches (25 cm) deep for the furnace. Aim the tuyere of the blower down into the pit at an angle of 15 degrees. Build the walls of the furnace with mud made from the excavated soil mixed with water (B). The walls should be 10 inches (25 cm) above the ground. Let it dry until the mud stiffens.

3. Light a fire (see page 33) in the furnace with wood and let it burn for about 1 hour to preheat (C).

4. Fill the furnace to the top with charcoal.

5. Start blowing the furnace with the blower: adjust the rate so that 3 handfuls (about 1 pound [500 g]) of charcoal are consumed every 5 to 7 minutes (D).

6. Add about 10 pellets of ore (about 7 ounces [200 g] ore) on top of each charge of charcoal. Repeat until you've used up all of the ore.

UPDRAFT KILN

TIPS

Roll your clay into a "snake" about ⅓ inch (1 cm) thick. Coil the snake around a finger. If it doesn't break apart completely, then it is suitable for pottery.

If the clay does start to crack while it's drying in the fire, use a stick to smear it with "grog," a paste of fibrous plant materials such as bark fiber. Finely crushed sand or old pottery also works.

A kiln is a type of furnace for heating materials, in which the fuel is kept separate from the objects being heated. It consists of a firebox at ground level where the fuel is burned and an insulated chamber above this where the objects to be heated are placed. Wood is burned in the firebox, and flames rise by natural draft into the ware chamber via holes in the floor and then exit through the top of the kiln. The temperature is less variable within a kiln than in a simple fire pit, so pottery baked in a kiln is less likely to crack from thermal shock. I started making kilns as a means of experimenting with metals, but the quality of my pottery improved when I started firing it in a kiln.

TOOLS AND MATERIALS

Digging Stick (page 20)

Water

Pots (for carrying water)

Clay (for the perforated kiln floor and the grate bars of the firebox)

1. Use the digging stick to dig a trench 20 inches (50 cm) wide, 20 inches (50 cm) deep, and 20 inches (50 cm) long into the side of a slope so that it is well drained. This will form the firebox of the kiln (A).

2. Use the digging stick to mix the excavated soil with water to make mud. Build a mud wall in the middle of the trench up to ground level and let it dry.

3. Use the digging stick to carve an opening in this wall once it is solid to act as the entrance of the firebox (B).

4. Build mud walls for the kiln in a cylinder shape, 20 inches (50 cm) wide and 20 inches (50 cm) tall (C).

HOW TO USE A KILN

Stack the kiln with dry pottery to be fired; cover the pottery with broken potsherds or flat tiles made for this purpose. Collect dry wood up to 3 times the weight of the pottery. Start a fire (see page 33) in the firebox; feed sticks through the grate bars. Add just enough wood to heat the kiln, not so much that black smoke billows out of the top. Adding too much wood at one time will choke the kiln and cool it down. Look through the top of the kiln to monitor the firing; it will usually take between 3 and 4 hours. When all the pots are glowing at least red-hot they will be ready; however, continuing to fire them at higher temperatures will make them stronger. Block the firebox entrance with sold and rocks to prevent cold air from getting in; let the pottery cool slowly to avoid cracking.

5. Make a clay disk 20 inches (50 cm) in diameter to form the floor of the kiln; poke holes in it with your fingers or the digging stick (D). Let it dry and then place the perforated disk in the kiln so it sits over the firebox.

6. Make grate bars about 20 inches (50 cm) long out of clay for the firebox; let them dry. Place them horizontally in the firebox so that they are halfway between the floor and roof of the firebox (E).

HOW TO MAKE CERAMICS

Ceramics can be made with charcoal (see page 171), but firing in a kiln is more efficient, and the pots won't break as easily.

Water

Clay (see Tips, page 176)

Updraft Kiln (page 176)

Dry wood

Fire (see page 33)

1. Wet the clay and knead it to an even consistency. Pick out any stones and sticks.

2. Pick up the clay and slam it down, folding it each time to remove air bubbles.

3. Form a pot from the clay: coil or pinch the clay into the shape of a pot. Repeat until you have used all of the clay.

4. Dry the pots completely; this could take a few days, depending on the weather. Dry them next to a fire if there is no sun.

5. When the pots are bone-dry, stack them tightly into the kiln.

6. Start a fire in the firebox of the kiln and periodically feed wood into the firebox. It could take 3 to 4 hours for a small kiln to reach the necessary high temperature.

7. After all the pots have glowed at least red-hot, allow the fire to go out and let the pots cool overnight inside the kiln. Take them out of the kiln the next day.

NATURAL DRAFT FURNACE

HOW TO USE THE NATURAL DRAFT FURNACE

Light the furnace by pouring hot coals through the top. Add more wood through the top until the furnace is full of burning-hot coals. When the furnace is burning white hot as seen through the air pipe, add any materials to be melted through the top of the furnace. Alternate layers of wood and ore. The furnace gets incredibly hot and will fuse and sinter sand as well as melt ore. It should be able to smelt iron from its ore.

A natural draft furnace is basically a chimney that increases the draft of the fire via the stack effect. The height of the chimney and the temperature difference between the furnace gases and the ambient air create a pressure differential that causes air to be drawn into the furnace. The air-pulling effect is similar to the lifting effect of a hot-air balloon. It can be quite strong and negate the use of a bellows provided the stack is high enough and resistance in the fuel bed is sufficiently low. It can be used for smelting iron, though I've not done this before. I did manage to melt ore to produce slag, and this was done with wood fuel instead of charcoal.

TOOLS AND MATERIALS

Digging Stick (page 20)

Water

Pots (for carrying water)

Fibrous material, such as grass or bark fiber (for enriching the mud; add sand if the clay is too pure)

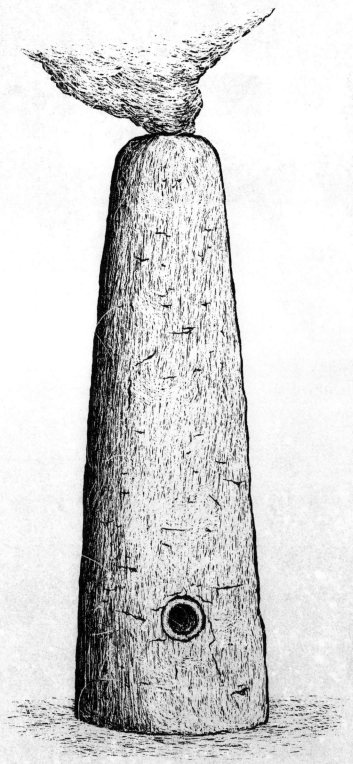

1. Use the digging stick to excavate soil; mix the soil with water and fibrous material to form mud.

2. Build a mud wall around a circle 10 inches (25 cm) in diameter. The wall should be 5 inches (12.5 cm) thick. Do this by molding the mud by hand. Keep adding layers to form a tall cylinder, waiting for each layer to dry slightly until stiff enough to build the next layer without slumping. Make it 6 feet (1.75 m) high (A).

3. When partially dry, that is to say unlikely for the mud to slump, dig a door into the front of the furnace. Make the door at least 5 inches (12.5 cm) wide and 10 inches (25 cm) tall.

4. Make a clay air pipe 3 inches (7.5 cm) in diameter and about 10 inches (25 cm) long (B). When dry, close in the entrance of the furnace with mud and put the air pipe in at the top of the doorway to let air into the furnace.

FORGE BLOWER

A centrifugal blower is a fan with paddles whose plane is in line with the rotor. When the fan is spun, air is thrown outward from the paddles while low pressure near the rotor draws in more air to replace it. Housing can be added so that the fan inside sucks in air through a hole at the top of the housing while exiting air is directed out of a pipe instead of being thrown out radially. This blower works whether the fan is spun clockwise or counterclockwise. Power it with a bow or a cord drawn backward and forward. A legal restriction on hunting in my area prompted me to develop this means of blowing air into furnaces instead of using a leather bellows. This simple air pump is more efficient than the more commonly used leather pot or bag bellows. There's a lesson here: inventions can be useful by-products of restrictions.

TOOLS AND MATERIALS

Hand Axe (page 18)

Wood (for the rotor and frame)

Thin, flat material such as stiff bark or light but strong leaves (for the fan blades)

Bark fiber or vines (for lashing)

Clay (for building the housing)

Stone Blades (page 16)

1 flat stone (for forming the socket the rotor will sit in)

Cordage (page 76) made from bark fiber (for powering the rotor)

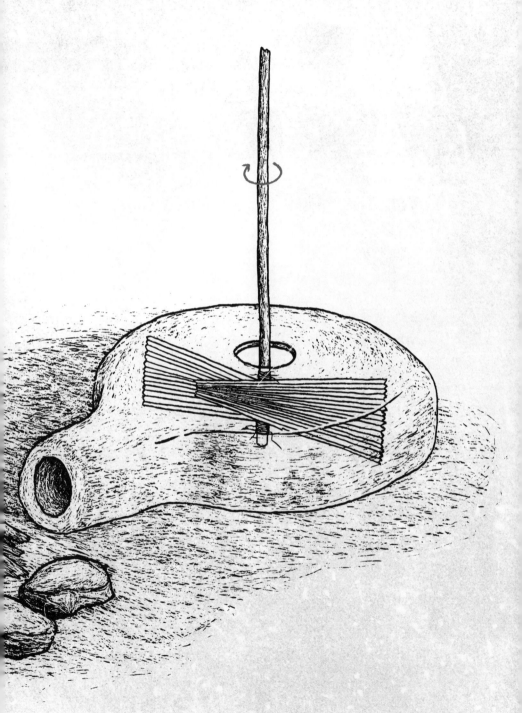

1. Use the hand axe to cut a piece of wood for the rotor.

2. Use the hand axe to split the wood and put the fan blade into it (A). Use bark fiber or vines to lash it up.

3. Flatten the clay into a disk a little larger than the fan (B).

4. Add a protrusion so that the disk resembles a flat raindrop with the point cut off (C). This will form the spout of the housing.

5. Make a hole in the center of the disk (D). This will be the housing's air entry. It should be roughly equal in size to the air exit (air in should be equal to air out).

6. Use more clay to build up the sides of the housing. As you do so, form the air exit into a round pipe. It may help to use a round log as a form. Make the walls of the blower a bit larger than the width of the fan blades (E).

7. When the housing is finished, let it dry and then turn it over (it was constructed upside down).

No bottom is required: the open bottom is the ground.

8. Use a stone blade to carve a hole in the flat stone to form the socket the rotor will sit in. Place the flat stone on the ground (F).

9. Put the rotor and fan into the housing so that the rotor is sticking out of the hole in the top of the housing.

10. Place the rotor and housing over the stone so that the bottom of the rotor sits in the socket.

11. To power the rotor, hold the rotor between the palms of your hands and rapidly spin it. If using a cord to power the rotor, use the stone blade to carve a notch in the top of the rotor and put the middle of the cord through this notch. Wrap the cord around the rotor and pull the ends outward rapidly. The rotor will spin in one direction and the momentum will coil the cord back around it to be spun in the other direction. Cords will only work with heavy fan blades (like those made of bark).

ACKNOWLEDGMENTS

There were many people who helped make this book a reality. Thank you to my agents, Eve Attermann and Jaime Carr, who enjoyed my channel and believed that there was a book here.

Thank you to Zachary Smith and Ben Neale for the illustrations and photos that have made this book look awesome.

A huge thanks to my publishing team at Clarkson Potter—Jenni Zellner, Angelin Borsics, Craig Adams, Kim Tyner, Mark McCauslin, Maureen Clark, Ellie Maddock, Jen Wang, Doris Cooper, and Aaron Wehner—for bringing this book to life.

And above all, thank you to the fans, who have supported me and my channel from the beginning.

ABOUT THE AUTHOR

John Plant is a thirty-six-year-old Australian citizen living in far north Queensland who has a keen interest in making things from scratch in the wild, without modern tools or materials. He studied science at James Cook University in Cairns and had various jobs, including a lawn mowing run. He started the YouTube channel Primitive Technology in 2015 as a means of sharing his interest online with like-minded people. The channel became an international success thanks to the straightforward presentation of primitive techniques combined with the absence of talking or narration, appealing to people of all languages and cultures.